CALLED TO SERVE

THE HISTORICAL SERIES OF THE REFORMED CHURCH IN AMERICA
NO. 102

CALLED TO SERVE
Essays on RCA Global Mission

Editors: **Charles E. Van Engen**
Jean Van Engen
Sally Tapley

REFORMED CHURCH PRESS
Grand Rapids, Michigan

Printed in the United States of America

ISBN: 978-1-950572-13-7

Library of Congress Control Number: 2020949675

Left to right: Sally Tapley, Chuck and Jean Van Engen

Chuck and Jean Van Engen served as RCA missionaries in Chiapas, Mexico, in theological education, developing women and men as leaders for Spanish-speaking churches. They are the founders of Latin American Christian Ministries that provides doctoral studies in theology for Latin American scholars. Sally Tapley served for many years as a Member of the Board of Trustees of the Southern Normal School in Brewton, Alabama, and has participated in multiple RCA committees and task forces. She is an ordained elder in the RCA.

The Historical Series of the Reformed Church in America

The series was inaugurated in 1968 by the General Synod of the Reformed Church in America acting through the Commission on History to communicate the church's heritage and collective memory and to reflect on our identity and mission, encouraging historical scholarship which informs both church and academy.

www.rca.org/series

General Editor
    James Hart Brumm, MDiv, MPhil
    New Brunswick Theological Seminary

Associate Editor
    Jeffrey Chu, MDiv
    Grand Rapids, MI

Copy Editor
    Joshua Parks
    Grand Rapids, MI

Production Editor
    Russell L. Gasero
    Archives, Reformed Church in America

Cover Design
    Matthew Gasero
    Archives, Reformed Church in America

General Editor Emeritus
    Donald J. Bruggink, PhD, DD
    Van Raalte Institute, Hope College

Commission on History
    Alexander Arthurs, Western Theological Seminary
    Lynn Japinga, PhD, Hope College
    Andrew Klumpp, MDiv, Southern Methodist University
    Steven Pierce, DMin, Grand Rapids, MI
    David M. Tripold, PhD, Monmouth University
    David Zomer, MDiv, Kalamazoo, MI

Contents

Notes on the Contributors

Alan Beagley and Jeanette Beagley-Koolhaas, both Reformed Church in America (RCA)-ordained ministers, are Fuller Theological Seminary graduates who served as missionary teachers in Taiwan. Jeanette's service encompassed the years of 1978 to 1994, including several years as a volunteer, while Alan was in Taiwan from 1986 to 1994. They were co-pastors of Williston Park Reformed Church in New York from 1997 to 2003. Jeanette served as the ThM program director at Western Theological Seminary from 2006 to 2014.

James Hart Brumm is the director of the Reformed Church Center, the Theological Writing Center, and the Seminary Archives at New Brunswick Theological Seminary. The editor of five books and author of a monograph, three books, numerous articles and essays, and about 350 hymns, he serves as general editor of The Historical Series of the Reformed Church in America.

William DeBoer, a graduate of Western Theological Seminary, and his wife Peg worked for eleven years at Cook Christian Training School, an inter-denominational, inter-tribal school in Arizona whose mission was to train Native Americans for church careers. This was followed by ten years serving as RCA missionaries among the Ch'ol Mayan language group in Chiapas, Mexico. After pastoring the Jicarilla Apache Reformed Church in northern New Mexico for seventeen years, Bill and Peg retired to Arizona.

Linda Walvoord deVelder is a graduate of Hope College and has a PhD from the University of Chicago. She has taught writing and literature at various colleges, and she retired in 2014 from the University of Cincinnati. She currently lives in Holland, Michigan. She married John deVelder (now deceased), the son of Walter deVelder, an RCA missionary to China and Asia. Together, they studied the Amoy mission work in which his family and some of Linda's ancestors were involved.

Eugene Heideman, a minister in the RCA, served as a missionary in the Church of South India from 1960 to 1970, and as the secretary for world mission for the Reformed Church in America from 1982 to 1994. He was on the faculty of Central College in Pella, Iowa, from 1970 to 1976 and of Western Theological Seminary in Holland, Michigan, from 1976 to 1982. He retired in 1984 and now lives in Holland, Michigan.

J. Samuel Hofman is an ordained minister of the RCA. He and his wife Helen spent forty-two years as RCA missionaries in Chiapas, Mexico, working in leadership development, materials development, and translation with the Tzeltal and Tojolabal Mayan groups. The Hofmans are retired in Holland, Michigan.

John Hubers and his wife, Lynne, served as RCA missionaries in the Arabian Gulf for twelve years. John was also the supervisor of RCA mission work in the Middle East and South Asia for five years and taught missiology at Northwestern College in Orange City, Iowa, for nine and a half years. John and Lynne are currently serving as RCA missionaries at the Mekane Yesus Seminary in Addis Ababa, Ethiopia.

Derrick Jones is the supervisor of RCA mission programs in Africa. He has served one senior pastorate in New York City and two assistant pastorates in Washington, DC. He is a graduate of Princeton Theological Seminary and is passionate about meaningful mission engagements in Africa that promote transformation and sustainability.

LeRoy Koopman is an RCA-ordained pastor who served for many years as an editor and writer for the RCA denominational staff. He has written and published many Bible studies and other books. His book *Taking the Jesus Road: The Ministry of the Reformed Church in America Among Native Americans* was written for the RCA Historical Series and is the source of much of the information in chapter six of this volume.

Gordon D. Laman served as a missionary in Japan for forty-three years. Working in partnership with the Japanese church, his early duties variously included those of district evangelist, developer of media evangelism and Bible correspondence courses, and pastor. Subsequently, he served for twenty-one years as a member of the faculty of Tokyo Union Theological Seminary as director of field education, teaching courses in Asian mission and communication while traveling throughout Japan as an itinerant evangelist on weekends.

Jacob Moss served as the executive director of Jackson County Ministries/Grace Covenant Ministries (GCM) from 2004 to 2017. Since 2017, he is continuing to help GCM as director of development. He and his wife, Sharon, are now residing in Orange City, Iowa.

Richard Otterness had his first exposure to global mission as a young adult short-term volunteer in Taiwan. After serving as pastor with three congregations in upstate New York, he worked as synod executive for Albany Synod, where he encouraged missional commitments by congregations. In 2006, he and his wife, Carolyn, moved to Hungary, where they served as RCA missionaries for twelve years.

Sally Tapley has served on many committees and boards related to ministries of the Reformed Church in America. She was a member of the General Program Council for six years and served as a member of the Board of Trustees of the Southern Normal School for ten years, representing the Reformed Church. Sally is an ordained elder in the RCA.

Charles (Chuck) E. Van Engen is the Arthur F. Glasser Senior Professor Emeritus of Biblical Theology of Mission in the School of Intercultural Studies at Fuller Theological Seminary, where he taught from 1988 to 2015. Chuck was born and raised in Chiapas, Mexico, of RCA missionary parents. Both Chuck and his wife, Jean, are graduates of Hope College. In Chiapas, they founded a seminary and were involved in extension theological education, leadership formation, women's ministries, and training evangelists for the National Presbyterian Church of Mexico from 1973 to 1985. They are the founders of the Latin American Christian Ministries, which provides doctoral studies in theology for Latin American scholars. Chuck served as president of General Synod in 1997–98. The parents of three grown children, Chuck and Jean live in Holland, Michigan.

Jean Van Engen and her husband Chuck spent twelve years in Chiapas ministering with Spanish-speaking churches, developing leaders for the churches and among women. For eighteen years, Jean worked as a research business administrator at City of Hope Comprehensive Cancer Center in Duarte, California. She has also served as the chief financial officer for Latin American Christian Ministries since its inception in 2000.

Foreword

Charles E. Van Engen

The purpose of this book is to briefly tell the story of the Reformed Church in America's (RCA) actions in global intercultural mission during the past 180 years, especially focused on how the RCA began its mission endeavors in different parts of the world. Some time ago, it came to the attention of the editors of this book that many pastors, leaders, and members of RCA churches in North America had little or no knowledge of the RCA's long pilgrimage of mission action around the world. In part, this is because women and men graduating from RCA seminaries, pastors trained in other seminaries, members of RCA church mission task forces, deacons, elders, staff members, and leaders in RCA congregations have not had easy access to this story.

There are a number of large, well-researched, clearly written books dealing with the RCA's intercultural mission in countries around the world. We will include references to these larger works at the ends of various chapters of this book. Here, we hope to offer you a series of brief glimpses of how the RCA became involved in mission endeavors in various parts of the world, who were the first RCA missionaries sent there, what kinds of activities they did, and what the fruit of that work looks like today.

As editors of this volume, we want to express our deep appreciation and gratitude to the authors of these chapters. This has been a wonderful experience for us. Every person whom we invited some months ago to write a brief chapter accepted our invitation. Everyone so graciously accepted the editorial touches we gave each chapter. Many other RCA folks helped us find photos that we could include in these chapters. We are grateful for the encouragement and support that the RCA Historical Series gave us in preparing this book for publication.

CHAPTER 1

Witnesses of God's Mission

Charles E. Van Engen

Therefore, since we are surrounded by so great a cloud of witnesses, let us also lay aside every weight and the sin that clings so closely, and let us run with perseverance the race that is set before us, looking to Jesus the pioneer and perfecter of our faith, who for the sake of the joy that was set before him endured the cross, disregarding its shame, and has taken his seat at the right hand of the throne of God.[1]

The setting that the author of Hebrews had in mind was a large stadium where the runners were being viewed and cheered on by the "witnesses." The Greek here is *nephos marturon* (νέπηοσ μαρτύρων), a great "cloud of witnesses," a multitude of spectators who hover over the stadium like a cloud. They are watching and witnessing the race.

Who are these witnesses? Whom does the writer of Hebrews have in mind? The adverb "therefore" in verse 1 gives us a clue. The writer is thinking of all those listed in the previous chapter (Hebrews 11:4-40). Some biblical scholars have called these folks the "heroes of the faith." But the author of Hebrews does not portray them as heroes. Rather, they are "aliens and strangers on earth" (11:13) whose "weakness was

---

[1]   Hebrews 12:1-2 (NRSV).

turned to strength" (11:34). They were tortured and flogged, chained, imprisoned, stoned, and even "sawed in two" (11:35-37). In fact, the author of Hebrews asserts that the people of the cloud need the readers of the book of Hebrews so that together they can be "made perfect" (11:40).

In other words, in God's mission, God does extraordinary things through the faith of the ordinary people listed in Hebrews 11. "Therefore," the writer of Hebrews exhorts us, "since we are surrounded by such a cloud of witnesses, let us...run with perseverance the race marked out for us" (12:1).

In this book, we want to tell you, the reader, about women and men who are part of the "cloud of witnesses" who surround us. These are the ordinary women and men through whom God did extraordinary things. And as a way to prepare you to read the rest of the book, in this first chapter I want to offer you a glimpse of four groups of "witnesses." As you and I stand on the racetrack in the center of the stadium, we look up at the spectators and can distinguish four different groups. They represent four aspects of the RCA's history of intercultural mission action. As you read the rest of this book, I invite you to watch for these four groups of witnesses and see how they took part in the RCA's mission endeavors in various parts of the world.

The RCA was among the first to send long-term, international, intercultural missionaries from North America to other parts of the world.

The RCA was among the first to send long-term, international, intercultural missionaries from North America to other parts of the world.

The first group includes those who were the first missionaries to be sent out by the RCA from North America to other parts of the world. I will offer you some select examples because there are too many to list them all.

The RCA's intercultural missionary activity began almost as soon as the Dutch Reformed immigrants arrived on the east coast of North America. One of the most noteworthy early Dutch Reformed missionary pastors was the Reverend Johannes Megapolensis (1601–70). In 1642, Megapolensis immigrated from the Netherlands to what is today Albany, New York. There, he befriended the native Mohawk people of the northern Hudson River Valley, and by 1643 he was preaching fluently in Mohawk. In 1644, he sent to the Netherlands a document that described the Mohawks' language, costumes, religion and government. Many Mohawks became Christians and joined as members of the Dutch Reformed Church in what is today the city of Albany in upper New York.[2] Megapolensis was the pastor of that church for six years. Later, as a pastor in New Amsterdam, he helped many slaves gain their freedom among the Dutch settlers. Sadly, after the English took over New Amsterdam and renamed it New York (1664), the friendship between the Dutch settlers and the Mohawks disintegrated, and almost all the Mohawks left the Dutch Reformed Church in the late 1600s and early 1700s.

Only three years after William Carey (1761–1834) left England for India, Dutch Reformed leaders in New York joined Presbyterians and Baptists to create the New York Missionary Society (1796) as an interdenominational missionary organization. In 1812, this cooperative mission organization joined several other denominations to form the American Board of Commissioners for Foreign Missions (ABCFM), of which the RCA was a member until 1857. In that year, the RCA's Board of Foreign Missions was incorporated in the state of New York, with the Rev. Theodore Frelinghuysen as its first president and Dr. Isaac Ferris the first secretary, well-known names in the history of the RCA. Note that by the time the RCA formed its own Board of Foreign Missions, RCA missionaries had been working for some years in India and China under the auspices of the ABCFM.

In cooperation with several other denominations involved in the ABCFM, the RCA was at the forefront of sending the first intercultural missionaries to a number of countries. The first of these were Dr. John and Harriet Scudder. John was a medical doctor with a successful medical practice in New York City, and he and Harriet were the first medical missionaries sent by the ABCFM in 1819. They first went to Ceylon (now Sri Lanka) and then to India. In 1853, John's sons founded the Arcot Mission of the Reformed Church in America in India. Over many years, John and Harriet's seven sons, eleven grandchildren, five great-grandchildren, and two great-great grandchildren all served as missionaries in India. A granddaughter, Dr. Ida Sophia Scudder (1870–1960) founded the Vellore Hospital, School of Nursing, and Medical School, which to this day is one of the premier medical training centers in India.[3]

---

[2] The town was originally called Rensselaerswyck and was later named Albany by the English.
[3] Gerald H. Anderson, ed., *Biographical Dictionary of Christian Missions* (Grand Rapids, MI: Eerdmans, 1998), 609–10.

The first North American missionary to be sent to Canton, China, in 1829–30 was David Abeel (1804–46). He was sent by the RCA through ABCFM. He was an 1826 graduate of New Brunswick Theological Seminary (NBTS). In 1833, for health reasons, David Abeel returned to the U.S. via Europe, speaking on behalf of global mission. He did extensive preaching, speaking, and writing about world mission, especially in Reformed churches.[4] In 1844, he established the Amoy mission of the RCA in China together with Elihu Doty and William John Pohlman. He motivated many young people to commit themselves to global mission. In England, he was instrumental in forming the Society for Promoting Female Education in the East, the first women's foreign mission group to be organized.[5]

Horace Grant Underwood (1859–1916), a graduate of New Brunswick Theology Seminary, was ordained in the RCA in 1884. Underwood went to Korea under the Presbyterians in 1885. Four generations of the Underwood family served as missionaries in Korea. Horace G. Underwood started a Christian orphanage in Seoul, founded the Saemunan Presbyterian Church, began the Korean Tract Society, published the first Korean hymnal, and chaired the board of translators of the Bible into Korean. He founded the Young Men's Christian Association (YMCA) in Seoul, began what became known as the Pierson University, and founded what is today the Yonsei University in Seoul, South Korea.[6]

This list of first missionary leaders would be incomplete without mentioning Samuel Marinus Zwemer (1867–1952). Born in Vriesland, Michigan, Zwemer was the son of an RCA pastor. Zwemer graduated from Hope Academy (1887) and NBTS (1890). In 1889, Zwemer and his friend James Cantine created the American Arabian Mission to support them as they headed for Arabia. They were the first Protestant missionaries sent from North America to the Middle East for mission work in an Islamic context. In 1894, the RCA accepted responsibility to sponsor them in their work among Muslims. Zwemer married Amy Elizabeth Wilkes in 1896. An evangelist, distributor of Bibles, writer, promoter, and speaker, Zwemer authored or co-authored 38 books. He was the principle editor of the journal *The Moslem World* for thirty-seven years. Zwemer also founded the American Mission Hospital in

---

4   Until 1869, the RCA was often referred to as the "Dutch Reformed Church" but was formally known as "The Reformed Protestant Dutch Church in North America" (RPDC).

5   Anderson, *Biographical Dictionary*, 1–2.

6   Anderson, *Biographical Dictionary*, 689.

Bahrain. From 1929 to 1937, Zwemer served as professor of missions at Princeton Theological Seminary.

In the following chapters, you will read of other women and men whom God used to begin RCA missionary endeavors in various places in the world. The people I chose to highlight above were selected because they represent how the RCA was at the forefront of mission-sending from North America to other parts of the world. RCA pastors, leaders, and churches nurtured, sent, and supported these first pioneer missionaries. They were ordinary people through whom the Holy Spirit did extraordinary things.

The RCA was unique in partnering with national churches.

Standing down on the field, as we look up at the stands of spectators, I would call your attention to a second group of witnesses: the leaders of national churches, denominations, and mission organizations outside North America with whom the RCA has partnered through the years. Once again, I will offer you some select examples that may help you recognize them as they are mentioned in subsequent chapters of this book.

In its global mission endeavors, the RCA has partnered with national churches around the world. During most of the nineteenth century, the Protestant denominations in North America sent their career missionaries to other countries in Asia, Africa, and Latin America with a mandate to form churches and church organizations that would be copies of, and belong to, the North American denomination. The assumed pattern was that, as new congregations were formed in India, China, Korea, and elsewhere, those congregations would be organized into districts, dioceses, presbyteries, or—in the language of the RCA—classes belonging to the American church. These were to be reproductions of the ecclesial structures of their mother churches in North America, with identical polities, under the authority and supervision of their American denominations.

Following that idea, in May of 1853, John Scudder and three of his sons, along with three native elders, officially formed the Classis of Arcot in southern India. As Eugene Heideman explains, "By virtue of that action, not only was the missionary activity of the Reformed Church established in that land, but [Tamil and Telugu-speaking] natives of India became members of the Protestant [Dutch] Reformed Church in America."[7]

---

[7]   Eugene Heideman, *A People in Mission: The Surprising Harvest* (New York: Reformed Church Press, 1980), 4.

Back in the United States, the General Synod of the RCA was delighted. Almost all North American Protestant denominational mission endeavors assumed that this colonial way of organizing the church in other parts of the world was the proper way to do things. In fact, until the middle of the twentieth century, this practice continued to be the norm in the mission work of many denominations around the world. The single, unique exception was the RCA. Here is the fascinating story.

Barely four years after the formation of the Classis of Arcot in India, the missionaries in China registered their disagreement. As Arie Brouwer recounts,

> The [1857] Synod...dealt with an elaborate document from the brethren at Amoy expressing their reluctance to form a classis there. Synod's committee protested that its missionaries had always been expected to develop churches in a form approaching, as nearly as possible, that of Reformed Protestant Dutch churches in our own land...The converts at Amoy, as at Arcot and elsewhere, [were] to be regarded as an integral part of [the American church]. The committee observed that the Presbyterians seemed to have no trouble with such an arrangement. They urged the brethren abroad to carry out the policy and directed [them] to apply to the Particular Synod of Albany to organize them into a classis....
>
> The missionaries in China disagreed. They maintained that organization as a classis would violate their [long] association with the English Presbyterian missionaries who had organized one-half of the six congregations at Amoy. They further pointed to the difficulty of carrying out judicial processes between America and China. The only way seemed to be recognition of an independent Chinese church.[8]

We need to remember that, at that time, a letter would take months to travel by boat from China to the United States. The discussion between the leaders of the RCA's General Synod and the Chinese missionaries actually went on for the next six years.

> Neither side would yield. The matter came to a head at the Synod of 1863. One of the [leading] missionaries at Amoy, John VanNest Talmage [was present at that Synod].... He argued for

8   Arie R. Brouwer, *Reformed Church Roots: Thirty-Five Formative Events* (New York: Reformed Church Press, 1977) 131.

the missionary point of view but was overcome by the opposition. Dr. Talbot W. Chambers, President of the Synod and Talmage's boyhood pastor...declared his unalterable opposition to Talmage's position.[9]

The missionaries in Amoy supported Talmage. They wrote to Synod: "It is not a matter of judgement only, but also of conscience. We conscientiously feel that in confirming such an organization we should be doing a positive injury and wrong to the churches of Christ established at Amoy, and that our duty to the Master and His people here forbids this."[10]

The discussion reached such a point that in 1864 the RCA missionaries in Amoy (more than 20 persons) stated that if Synod insisted on their forming a classis of the RCA in Amoy, Synod would need to recall all of them and send out others who agreed with Synod.[11] Finally, the RCA General Synod decided that, "In consideration of the peculiar circumstances of the Mission of Amoy, the brethren there are allowed to defer the formation of a Classis of Amoy until, in their judgment, such a measure is required by the wants and desires of the Churches gathered by them."[12]

In fact, the RCA missionaries in China never deemed it wise to form an RCA classis at Amoy, China. The commitment of the missionaries in China to support and partner with local and national churches became the assumed way the RCA would do mission everywhere in the world. Thirty years later, in 1902, the Classis of Arcot in India ceased to exist as a classis. The churches were transferred to the Synod of South India, made up of a number of Reformed churches working in the Arcot area. Eventually, in 1947, they joined Anglican, Methodist, Presbyterian, Congregational, and Reformed churches to form the Church of South India.

The important decision made by the General Synod in 1857 became the pattern—to this day—for all RCA long-term mission endeavors everywhere in the world. To my knowledge, the RCA's way of doing global mission is like no other denomination's international,

---

[9]   Brouwer, *Reformed Church Roots*, 131–32.

[10]   Brouwer, *Reformed Church Roots*, 132.

[11]   The RCA may be one of the only denominations whose missionaries at one point in time were essentially on strike.

[12]   Brouwer, *Reformed Church Roots*, 133. See also Herman Harmelink III, "World Mission," in *Piety and Patriotism*, ed. James W. Van Hoeven (Grand Rapids, MI: Eerdmans, 1976), 83–84.

cross-cultural mission work. Since 1857, the RCA has never planted its own RCA congregations, nor created its own denominational structures anywhere in the world. Rather, the RCA has always partnered with national, indigenous churches whose local leaders have created their own ecclesial structures appropriate to their cultural contexts. The RCA has partnered with national churches in India, China, Taiwan, the Philippines, Mexico, and various countries in Africa and Europe.

Please notice this unique feature in the chapters of this book. One of the results of this aspect of RCA interdenominational mission is that the RCA, as small as it is, has often served as a catalyst to mobilize other larger denominations and mission organizations in new, creative, and significant mission ventures. To this day, partnership in mission is an integral part of the RCA's way of doing mission.

The RCA was among the first to join and participate in multi-denominational, ecumenical organizations.

As we look up at the spectators in the stadium, I would point out a third group of witnesses. These are the ecumenical, cooperative organizations and their leaders with whom the RCA has collaborated in various parts of the world. This group represents a third historical feature of RCA mission: its commitment to multidenominational and ecumenical cooperation as championed by the missionaries.

During the nineteenth and early twentieth centuries, there were two pathways or arenas by which world evangelization and mission influenced the development of trans-denominational, ecumenical cooperation. One road was laid out primarily by young people and eventuated in the RCA's membership and participation in cooperative, multi-denominational organizations in the U.S. and Canada committed to global mission support and sending. Earlier, I mentioned the American Board of Commissioners for Foreign Missions (ABCFM), the most significant mission society in the U.S. of the nineteenth century. Due to the initiative of students from Williams College and Andover Seminary, the ABCFM was incorporated in 1812 and included representatives from Congregationalist, Presbyterian, and Reformed traditions. The RCA was an integral part of the ABCFM. John Scudder and David Abeel were sent and supported by the ABCFM. To give us an idea of the size of this mission organization, by the time of its centennial in 1910, the ABCFM was responsible for 102 mission stations globally and a missionary staff of 600 working in India, Ceylon, West Central Africa (Angola), South Africa and Rhodesia, Turkey, China, Japan,

Micronesia, Hawaii, the Philippines, Mexico, Spain, Austria, and Native tribes in North America.

Another very important trans-denominational mission organization that formed toward the end of the nineteenth century was the Student Volunteer Movement for Foreign Missions (SVM). The SVM was created by college students who had been active in the Young Men's Christian Association (YMCA), the Young Women's Christian Association (YWCA) and the Inter-Seminary Missionary Alliance.[13] In 1888, John R. Mott organized the YMCA chapter at Cornell in New York.

From February 26 through March 1, 1891, the first International Convention of the SVM gathered in Cleveland, Ohio. The motto of the convention was "The Evangelization of the World in this Generation," and this became the foundational watchword of the SVM and the basis for the great World Missionary Conference convened in 1910 in Edinburgh, Scotland. According to the 1891 convention's report, 6200 students gathered in Cleveland committed to world evangelization, from 500 academies, 175 normal schools, 5000 theological seminaries, 1200 colleges, 125 medical colleges, and 100 training schools.[14] Eighty percent were under thirty years of age. One-third were women. And they belonged to Presbyterian, Methodist, Baptist, Congregational, Lutheran, Episcopal, Friends, and "other denominations." Three names are mentioned in the report as associated with the RCA: the Rev. H. N. Cobb from the Board of Foreign Missions of the Reformed Church in America and student volunteers H. Huizinga and H. Vanderploeg from Hope College.[15] Samuel Zwemer (1867–1952) was inspired and nurtured by the SVM as he began his pioneering missionary work in Arabia in 1889.

The SVM was the parent institutional network that eventually gave rise to large global ecumenical organizations like the International Missionary Council (IMC) and the World Council of Churches (WCC), among others. In the late 1940s and early 1950s, leaders from the SVM also began student mission networks like the InterVarsity Urbana Student Missions Conferences, which now gather 12,000 to 16,000 students every three years for Bible study, prayer, shared vision, and personal commitment to world evangelization.

[13]   The YMCA and YWCA were originally founded in England in 1844 as student evangelism and mission organizations.

[14]   *Report of the First International Convention of the Student Volunteer Movement for Foreign Missions 1891*, reprint (Pasadena, CA: William Carey Library, 1979).

[15]   *Report*, 188, 199.

A second stream of missionary influence to create global trans-denominational cooperation flowed from the wellspring of cross-cultural missionaries who sought ways to cooperate with other denominations and Christian groups in the countries where they worked. Earlier, I mentioned the story of the RCA's missionaries in China who did just that. They were not alone. During the past 150 years, RCA missionaries have been active participants in the creation of multi-denominational associations of churches all over the world. Many of these associations flowed naturally from the RCA's history of mission partnerships with national churches, as I summarized earlier in this chapter.

As you read the rest of this book, notice how often these multidenominational cooperative endeavors are mentioned. For instance, the churches that were the fruit of the RCA's missionary work in the Arcot area of southern India eventually became members of the Church of South India, founded in 1947. In Japan, the RCA's ministries became part of the United Church of Christ in Japan, Kyodan (founded in 1941). In Ethiopia, the RCA has worked closely with the Ethiopian Evangelical Church Mekane Yesus (founded in 1959). In other parts of Africa, the RCA has cooperated with the Africa Inland Church, among others. RCA missionaries have worked with the Baptists in Burma and with the Presbyterians in Korea. In Taiwan, the RCA has worked with the Presbyterians. In Chiapas, Mexico, the RCA worked closely with the National Presbyterian Church of Mexico (founded in 1872). In Honduras and Nicaragua, the RCA has worked with the Moravian Church.

RCA missionaries have also been personally involved in interdenominational and multi-denominational mission agencies like Wycliffe Bible Translators, the United Bible Societies, Missionary Aviation Fellowship, Church World Service, and CEPAL in Nicaragua, among others.

Ecumenical, multidenominational cooperation flowed directly from the relationships and cooperative work of missionaries as a result of their missionary vision and commitment. These relationships flourished when they were centered around a vision for, and commitment to, world evangelization and gospel proclamation in word and deed.

The RCA was led in new mission ventures by the women of the church.

As we stand down on the field and look up at the stands, we see that the fourth group of witnesses is made up of women. This group is huge. They take up more than half of the stadium seats. I can only mention a few select examples whose stories may help you recognize them as they appear in subsequent chapters of this book.

The women of the RCA were key organizers, supporters, senders, and missionary personnel whom the RCA sent everywhere in the world. R. Pierce Beaver called them "the first feminist movement in North America,"[16] and Don Luidens called them "the rest of the story."[17] It is certainly the neglected and somewhat untold side of the history of RCA mission since 1800. The omission is all the more glaring when you consider the extent, scope, depth, and clarity of the mission vision, motivation, and organization which RCA women provided to further the cause of global mission. Most achievements in RCA mission-sending during the past 180 years would have been seriously curtailed, if not impossible, if it had not been for the contribution of the women of the church. "No other form of American intervention overseas has made a more powerful cultural impact than [the work of women in global and local mission] for women and children [everywhere in the world]."[18]

The story begins in 1802 at the dining table of Deacon John Simpkins and his wife, Mehitable, as told by R. Pierce Beaver:

> A guest raised his wine glass, admired the color and bouquet of the beverage, and exclaimed. This excellent wine probably costs a penny a glass. Just think if we would each forgo one glass tonight, the sum saved would buy several gospels or more tracts. Should we and our friends do without some little thing each week and save a cent, think of the hundreds of Bibles and hymnbooks with which missionaries could be supplied in just one year's time! The Deacon was treasurer of the Massachusetts Missionary Society. Then and there was born the idea of the Cent Society. Mrs. Simpkins agreed to be the collector, and she would transmit the collections to her husband for the use of the Society of which he was the treasurer.
>
> Women were already giving their pennies for missions, and the Cent Society brought forth a flood of copper coins. The immediate appeal of the new proposal probably lay in the fact

---

[16]   R. Pierce Beaver, *American Protestant Women in World Mission: A History of the First Feminist Movement in North America* (Grand Rapids, MI: Eerdmans, 1968).

[17]   Donald A. Luidens, "The Rest of the Story...: Hope Alumnae and International Missions," in *Into All the World: Hope College and International Affairs*, ed. Robert J. Donia and John M. Mulder (Holland, MI: Hope College, 1985).

[18]   Beaver, *American Protestant Women*, 9.

that one cent a week was about the sum almost any woman might be able to give if she denied herself some little thing. It appealed also to the widow's two mites of Jesus' parable, and the vision of the collective purchasing power of thousands of pennies made each single cent seem significant. It caught [their] imagination: Mrs. Simpkins was deluged by pennies.[19]

The Cent Societies became the foundation and backbone of early sending and support for global mission, including in the RCA.

> It was the Cent Societies with their simple membership requirements of dues of fifty-two cents a year which proliferated most rapidly and widely (first organized in 1804).... With the advent of foreign missions after 1810, the Cent Societies began contributing to the American Board of Commissioners for Foreign Missions (ABCFM) and then to the Baptist and United Foreign Missionary Societies (UFMS) when they began to send missionaries.... The Synod of the Reformed Church in America in 1822 requested the pastors and congregations to form auxiliaries of the UFMS and of the Synod's Committee on Domestic Missions. There were societies in both the Reformed and Presbyterian churches on Cedar Street in New York City. The Reformed Church promoted the Cent Societies not for foreign missions but for support of the Theological Seminary in New Brunswick.[20]

In 1825, the women of First Reformed Church in New Brunswick and the Reformed Church of Bedminster, New Jersey, organized to support mission. David Abeel encouraged the next step in the history of the participation of women in mission by promoting the separate organization of women's missionary work. In 1834, Abeel went to New York. There he influenced one of the most remarkable women in the history of the Protestant church in North America: Sara (Mrs. Thomas C.) Doremus (1802–77) of South Reformed Church in New York City. The mother of nine children, "Sarah was an active worker and leader in every aspect of women's concerns.... [At her initiative] the interdenominational Woman's Union Missionary Society (WUMS) of America was organized and incorporated in February of 1861. Mrs. Doremus remained president until her death in 1877.... [The WUMS

---

[19]   Beaver, *American Protestant Women*, 13–14.
[20]   Beaver, *American Protestant Women*, 19, 22, 39.

was] the first American non-denominational women's missionary society, whose object was to send single women as teachers and missionaries to Asia."[21]

Within a decade of its organization, the Woman's Union had its own missionaries and national workers in Burma, India, China, Syria, Greece, and Japan. Within 20 years of its founding, this organization had supported more than one hundred missionaries in twelve locations. Historian R. Pierce Beaver says, "It is the mother and inspiration of all those denominational societies and can claim a share in their achievements."[22]

The first denominational women's society was formed in 1868 as the New England Women's Foreign Missionary Society (Congregational) and later became the Women's Board of Missions (1869). Seven years later, the Women's Board of Missions of the RCA was formed. "Its purpose was 'to aid the Board of Foreign Missions of the Reformed Church in America by promoting its work among the women and children of heathen lands.' The Women's Board focused its efforts on raising funds and on increasing the size and strength of its local societies. [At its founding] there were already 19 such groups [in RCA churches], a few of which were of long standing."[23].

Even so, it was difficult at that time for women to gain a voice in the church's affairs. R. Pierce Beaver observes that,

> As late as the 1930s one of the oldest American churches (the RCA) still denied women a voice before its (synod). Miss Sue Weddell, the first woman executive secretary for missionary education, was at first forbidden to make a report to the Synod of the Reformed Church in America according to their policy. Happily the fathers and brethren wanted to hear the report, and they voted to waive that policy and permit her to speak....

---

[21] Anderson, *Biographical Dictionary*, 184. See also Nancy Hardesty, *Women Called to Witness: Evangelical Feminism in the 19th Century* (Nashville: Abingdon, 1984) 134; Ruth Tucker, *Guardians of the Great Commission: The Story of Women in Modern Missions* (Grand Rapids, MI: Zondervan, 1998), 76-77, 100; Una H. Ratmeyer, *Hands, Hearts, and Voices: Women Who Followed God's Call* (New York: Reformed Church Press, 1995), 2-3; Beaver, *American Protestant Women*, 90-91; Edwin Mulder, "Full Participation – A Long Time in Coming!" *Reformed Review* 17, no. 3 (1989): 225; and Brouwer, *Reformed Church Roots*, 147-48. Sarah Doremus and other contemporary women created numerous mission societies, sent and supported hundreds of women as missionaries around the world, and organized the first world missionary conference in 1900 in New York, ten years before the men met at Edinburgh, Scotland.

[22] Beaver, *American Protestant Women*, 92.

[23] Brouwer, *Reformed Church Roots*, 148.

During the short period of their existence [as autonomous women's sending societies] through 1882 sixteen women's societies reported total receipts of $5,940,045.00, a colossal sum in relation to the purchasing power of the dollar at the time. Thirty-five [mission] agencies had a combined income of $1,412,235 in 1900 alone. Income rose steadily. Receipts for 1923...totaled $1,008,942 for 8 Canadian women's societies. and $8,987,577 for 29 of the U.S. boards.[24]

In the RCA, the contributions of the Women's Board of Foreign Missions and the Women's Board of Domestic Missions had a major impact not only in international mission sending, but also in church extension in the United States. Arie Brouwer mentions their role in building parsonages, sending Christmas boxes, and supporting the clergy.[25] The Women's Board of Domestic Missions was also instrumental in beginning the Native American work with Frank Hall Wright (1895), the mission in Jackson County, Kentucky, through the ministries of Cora Smith and Nora Gant (1900), and the work in Chiapas, Mexico (Mrs. John Allen and Mrs. Tabor Knox, 1925).[26] You will read about the role of RCA women in these missionary endeavors in the chapters of this book.

The incredible hardships and challenges faced by the early pioneer missionary wives is a story in itself. Many missionary wives of the early nineteenth century lived short and painful lives compounded by the difficulty of travel, the presence of disease, the hardships of child-bearing, and the loneliness of isolation. In many cases, RCA women were aware of such suffering because of their key role in sending some of the first missionary couples through their support of the American Board of Commissioners for Foreign Missions. The women of the RCA were involved in David Abeel's going to China supported by the ABCFM in 1829. They supported John and Harriet Scudder's leaving for India in 1836. The support of the women's societies was crucial when Jacob Ennis, Elihu Doty, Elbert Nevius, and William Youngblood, together with their wives, left New York for China in 1836. They were accompanied by Azubah Caroline Condit (1810-44), the first single woman to engage in foreign missionary work first in Borneo and then

[24]   Beaver, *American Protestant Women*, 107, 109, 145-49.
[25]   Brouwer, *Reformed Church Roots*, 147-52.
[26]   See Eugene Heideman, *A People in Mission: Their Expanding Dream* (New York: Reformed Church Press, 1984), 31-38.

in Amoy, China.[27] A sister of Mrs. Nevius, Azuba studied Chinese and taught Chinese girls on Java. She started a boarding school for Chinese girls at Pontianak, Borneo, in 1842. Her early death cut short a promising missionary career.[28]

The story of missionary women, their efforts to win a place in world mission, the kinds of tasks they undertook, and their impressive achievements is a story that needs more research and recounting. R. Pierce Beaver, Ruth Tucker, Dana Robert, Nancy Hardesty, Una H. Ratmeyer and others have compiled much of the data. Examples in RCA mission history would include the names of Azubah Condit (Amoy, 1837), Caroline Adriance (Amoy, 1859), Mary Kidder (Japan, 1870), Lilly Duryee (China, 1894), Ida Scudder (India, 1900), Jeannette Veldman (China and the Middle East, 1927), and Wilma Kats (Sudan, 1948). Women like Mrs. Paul Van Cleef, Ruth Ransom, and Beth Marcus were very important and influential as mission organizers and administrators.

You see why there is such a crowd—a virtual cloud—in the stands of the stadium we are picturing. There are so many others who should be included.[29] Arie Brouwer states that from 1844 to 1925 some 245 women went out as missionaries under the auspices of the Reformed Church. In many cases, the work of missionary women had long-lasting impact. For example, Mrs. Elihu Doty was instrumental in founding the Amoy Girl's·School in 1847, one of the first girls' schools in China. In 1870, Mary Kidder began teaching Japanese girls, the start of the Ferris Seminary of Yokohama. As early as 1855, Mrs. Ezekiel Scudder began to teach Indian orphan girls, from which developed the Chittoor Female Seminary.[30] Later, Ida Scudder, along with several of her family members, founded the Vellore Hospital and Medical School in India.

Don Luidens states that from 1882 to 1961 there were seventy-five female Hope College graduates active in RCA mission.[31] Lewis R. Scudder III writes about RCA women who served in the Arabian Mission:

> The first single woman appointed to the Arabian Mission in 1902 was a nurse, Elizabeth DePree (who married James Cantine

[27] Heideman, *A People in Mission: Their Surprising Harvest*, 3–4.
[28] Anderson, *Biographical Dictionary*, 147.
[29] Una H. Ratmeyer has done us all a great service in compiling many of these stories in *Hands, Hearts, and Voices: Women Who Followed God's Call* (New York: Reformed Church Press, 1995).
[30] Brouwer, *Reformed Church Roots*, 148–50.
[31] Luidens, "The Rest of the Story," 70.

in 1904). Her appointment was quickly followed by that of Jane Scardefield (1903), Fanny Lutton (1904), Lucy Patterson (1904), Martha Vogel (1905), Minnie Wilterdink (1907), Dorothy Firman (1909), Christine Iverson (1909) Josephene Spaeth (1910), Sarah Hosmon (1911), Gertrud Shafheitlin (1912), and a whole train of remarkable individuals, most of whom remained with the mission for their whole careers. In the home station of Basrah up until World War I, work among Arab women was developed by Margaret Barny, Emma Worrall, Dorothy Van Ess, Martha Vogel, Christine Bennett, Elizabeth Calverley, and Jane Scardefield.[32]

The name of Mary Bruins Allison (1903–94) should be included here as well. A medical doctor, she devoted her life to serving women and families in the Arabian Gulf region. The history of the participation of RCA women in mission serves as an inspiration and example to encourage, challenge, and mobilize all of us for renewed, enthusiastic participation in the global mission of the Church.

An invitation to the reader

The writer of the book of Hebrews challenges us. Since we are surrounded by such a great cloud of witnesses some of whose names and faces we will see in this book, we are encouraged and called to "run with perseverance the race that is set before us, looking to Jesus the pioneer and perfecter of our faith."

The four groups of witnesses we have mentioned in this introductory chapter are examples of those in the RCA who have gone before us in global mission. We do not want to reenact the stories of the nineteenth-century American Protestant missionaries. But we can allow these stories to increase our vision and imagination, to inspire and challenge us. In a world of constant change, the call to carry the gospel to all those for whom Christ died has not changed. The needs of men, women, and children around the world are as great now as ever. Now that over 60 percent of all world Christianity is in the South and East of the globe, we need to find ways to develop new networks of partnerships, cooperative initiatives, and creative endeavors with our sisters and brothers around the globe. As you read the stories of the RCA's mission involvement in different parts of the world, I invite you to imagine how you will run the race. What extraordinary things might

32   Lewis R. Scudder III, *The Arabian Mission's Story In Search of Abraham's Other Son* (Grand Rapids, MI: Eerdmans, 1998), 203.

the Holy Spirit want to do in mission through ordinary people like you and me at this time of human history? We may be surprised. Together, let's "run with perseverance the race that is set before us, looking to Jesus the pioneer and perfecter of our faith."

For further reading

Anderson, Gerald H., ed. *Biographical Dictionary of Christian Missions.* Grand Rapids, MI: Eerdmans, 1998.

Beaver, R. Pierce. *American Protestant Women in World Mission: A History of the First Feminist Movement in North America.* Grand Rapids, MI: Eerdmans, 1968.

Brouwer, Arie R. *Reformed Church Roots: Thirty-Five Formative Events.* New York: Reformed Church Press, 1977.

Brown, Willard Dayton. "Development through Expansion at Home and Abroad." In *History of the Reformed Church in America,* 105-24. New York: Reformed Church in America Board of Publication, 1928.

Chamberlain, Mrs. William I. "The Church in Foreign Lands." In *Reformed Church in America Tercentenary Studies 1928: A Record of Beginnings,* 489-510. New York: Reformed Church in America, 1928.

Hardesty, Nancy. *Women Called to Witness: Evangelical Feminism in the 19th Century.* Nashville: Abingdon, 1984.

Harmelink, Herman, III. "World Mission." In *Piety and Patriotism,* edited by James W. Van Hoeven, 77-94. Grand Rapids, MI: Eerdmans, 1976.

Heideman, Eugene. *A People in Mission: The Surprising Harvest.* New York: Reformed Church Press, 1980.

Heideman, Eugene. *A People in Mission: Their Expanding Dream.* New York: Reformed Church Press, 1984.

Luidens, Donald A. "The Rest of the Story...: Hope Alumnae and International Missions." In *Into All the World: Hope College and International Affairs,* edited by Robert J. Donia and John M. Mulder, 69-81. Holland, MI: Hope College, 1985.

Mulder, Edwin. "Full Participation – A Long Time in Coming!" *Reformed Review* 17, no. 3 (1989): 224–46.

Ratmeyer, Una H. *Hands, Hearts, and Voices: Women Who Followed God's Call.* New York: Reformed Church Press, 1995.

Robert, Dana L. *American Women in Mission: A Social History of Their Thought and Practice.* Macon, GA: Mercer, 1996.

Rouse, Ruth and Stephen C. Neill, eds. *A History of the Ecumenical Movement 1517–1948 (2 vols.).* 3rd edition. Geneva: World Council of Churches, 1986.

Scudder, Lewis R., III, *The Arabian Mission's Story: In Search of Abraham's Other Son.* Grand Rapids, MI: Eerdmans, 1998.

Tucker, Ruth A. *Guardians of the Great Commission: The Story of Women in Modern Missions.* Grand Rapids, MI: Zondervan, 1988.

Van Engen, Charles, ed. *Principles of Partnership in Mission: A Case Study from Chiapas, Mexico.* Self-published, 2014. Originally published in *Reformed Review* 58, no. 1 (2004). Available at *https://repository. westernsem.edu/pkp/index.php/rr/issue/view/171.*

CHAPTER 2

India—1836

Eugene Heideman[1]

The Reformed Church mission in India began in partnership with the American Board of Commissioners for Foreign Missions

Dr. John Scudder was a rising star surgeon in New York City when he came across a pamphlet entitled *Conversion of the World, or The Claims of the 600,000,000 and the Ability and Duty of the Churches Respecting Them,* by Gordon Hall and the Rev. Samuel Newell, missionaries to Bombay. As he read it, he became convicted that he was called to be a missionary in response to the command to go into all the world to preach the gospel and heal the sick. After some time of thought and prayer with his wife Harriet, they were accepted as missionaries under the American Board of Commissioners for Foreign Missions (ABCFM), in association with the Reformed Church in America (RCA). In 1819, the RCA had no Board of Foreign Missions of its own. After a long sea voyage John and Harriet and their infant daughter arrived in Calcutta

---

[1]   The research, data, and information offered in this chapter is derived from Eugene Heideman, *From Mission to Church: The Reformed Church in America Mission to India,* The Historical Series of the Reformed Church in America (Grand Rapids, MI: Eerdmans, 2001).

Dr. John Scudder and
his wife Harriet

in October of 1819. Because the British East India Company would not permit American missionaries to work in India, the Scudders had to wait for passage to Ceylon (now Sri Lanka). While waiting, their little Maria died of dysentery. That was the first of many Reformed Church missionary deaths in India and Ceylon. Harriet gave birth in Ceylon to their second child, who died on February 25, 1820. The Scudders opened their new mission station in Panditeripo, Jaffna (in northern Ceylon), in July of 1820, among Tamil-speaking people.

John Scudder was the first Reformed Church medical missionary sent overseas. Because the ABFCM did not have the necessary funds, he opened his hospital and a school using his own funds. The government allowed them to use an old house with a thatched roof. Local people welcomed his ability to do cataract and other surgeries and to treat wounds. He and Harriet courageously cared for people suffering from typhoid, cholera and other tropical diseases. Harriet proved to be the ideal missionary wife and mother. Her third child died as an infant, after which they had ten children. Nine of them entered service as missionaries, while one, Samuel, died in America when he was a seminary student. During John's frequent evangelistic tours and medical clinics on tour, Harriet often had the care of forty people around her, including many who stayed in their home.

After the East India Company changed its policy to allow American missionaries to live in India, the Scudders moved to the city of Madras (now Chennai) on the coast of the Bay of Bengal. When they arrived there in 1836, there may have been as many as 20,000 Indo-European and Tamil Christians in the Madras area, so pioneering missionary John Scudder looked ninety miles inland to evangelize India. By 1853, the North Arcot District, approximately 160 miles long by fifty miles wide and centered on the towns of Arcot, Vellore, and Madanapalle, was recognized to be the responsibility of Reformed Church missionaries under the direction of the ABCFM. Thus, the beginning of RCA outreach in India was ecumenically Protestant in nature, as the RCA worked in cooperation with ABCFM missionaries in the Tamil- and Telegu-language regions of South India.

Partnerships in mission with other organizations

John Scudder was present at the 1850 Madras Missionary Conference, which was attended by six Wesleyan, three Church of Scotland, two Church of England, one Baptist, and four American missionaries. A central issue at the meeting was that of the role of observing caste distinctions among new converts at the time of baptism and the Lord's Supper. That was a crucial matter because a majority of converts were entering the church from the out-caste people who in Hindu society were not allowed to enter temples or associate and eat with the upper-caste people. The members present at the missionary conference recognized that the unity of the church was at stake. Scudder agreed with the decisions of the conference: (a) that candidates for baptism should be well instructed about the evils of caste and should be required to renounce caste usages both in principle and practice; (b) that renunciation of caste should be demanded of all Christians before coming to first communion; and (c) that all Christians, members and pastors, shall partake of a simple and suitable meal together, thus breaking caste. This decision became a basic principle of the Arcot Mission and the Classis of Arcot throughout the entire history of RCA mission in India.

RCA mission remained under the administration of the ABCFM until 1857, when the RCA formed its own Board of Foreign Missions. However, the ABCFM agreed already in 1853 to found the Arcot Mission, located in the North Arcot District, separately from its missions in Madurai and Madras. The general secretary of the ABCFM, Rufus Anderson, reminded the RCA missionaries of two basic principles. One was that if and when a church was organized in the Arcot area, it should not be subject to ecclesiastical control by any foreign mission agency or church. This principle reflects the practice of the Congregational church of which Anderson was a member. The RCA missionaries were in accord with Anderson on this point, but it was modified in accord with RCA polity when the RCA Classis of Arcot was founded on the same day as the Arcot Mission in 1853.

The second principle was that missionaries should focus on bringing individuals to faith and planting self-governing, self-supporting, self-propagating churches, a mission goal developed by Henry Venn and Rufus Anderson. When such churches came into existence, missionaries could consider themselves free to leave to serve in "regions beyond." This principle became a basic guideline for RCA mission policy.

The formation of these two bodies—the task-oriented Arcot Mission on the one hand and the ecclesiastical Classis of Arcot on the other—required the missionaries and church to define the respective responsibilities in relation to each other, while allowing for considerable overlapping of membership between them. In its first annual report, the Arcot Mission defined its basic function to be *the preaching of the gospel to the masses*. The report declared that the Arcot Mission did not intend to encumber itself by running educational institutions, medical clinics, or humanitarian agencies. Its second function was to compose and distribute tracts and books in the vernacular Indian language so that the voice of the gospel could be heard beyond the voices of missionaries and Indian evangelists. Its third function was to provide small schools for the instruction of Christian believers so that they would learn the way of the gospel, but it was not the purpose of the mission to provide schools for Hindu or Muslim children.

Alongside the Arcot Mission, the Classis of Arcot was formed to promote the life of the church according to the constitution of the Reformed Church in America. It was responsible for maintaining the teaching and good order of the church; guided by the Heidelberg Catechism, the Belgic Confession, and the Canons of Dort; and governed by ordained ministers, elders, and deacons of equal rank, without regard to whether they were missionary or Indian. The first Indian to be ordained to the office of minister was Andrew Sawyer in 1858. The Classis of Arcot was organized in accordance with the RCA General Synod's understanding at that time that RCA missionaries would form Reformed Churches overseas. However, when RCA missionaries in China objected and joined the Church of Christ in China, the Synod changed its policy. Thus, the Classis of Arcot was the only Reformed Church classis organized by action of the RCA world mission agency.

The Classis of Arcot was transferred to the South India United Church when it was formed in 1909.

The primary ministries completed by RCA missionaries in India

With their primary focus on preaching the gospel and calling people to be converted to Christ, the first generation of missionaries after John and Harriet Scudder were ordained male ministers: John and Harriet's sons William Waterbury, Jared Waterbury, and John Jr., plus William Chamberlain and Joseph Mayou. Their wives—respectively, Fanny, Elizabeth, and Julia Scudder and Charlotte Chamberlain and Margaret Mayou—were designated "assistant missionaries." A Scudder sister, Louisa, also served from 1856 to 1861 as an assistant missionary. The women were understood to be assisting their husbands in carrying out the primary calling to preach the gospel. Even when many educational and industrial/technical institutions and medical facilities opened, the Mission never ceased to emphasize that preaching the gospel remained its vital purpose. The Reformed Church Board of Foreign Missions began appointing women as "missionaries" in 1903.

Following the example of John Scudder, the ordained male missionaries were often away touring through the surrounding villages preaching the gospel, distributing scriptures and Christian literature, training evangelists, and encouraging new converts in the faith. Their wives remained at home rearing their families, supervising household staff, talking about family life and health with local women, and teaching wives of men being trained to be catechists. It was believed that the Christian family life of missionaries in itself was a valuable witness to the Christian faith.

As the number of converts grew and more Indian evangelist-catechists were trained to provide pastoral care and worship, missionary wives had to give more and more time to providing Christian instruction to their wives and their children. As the missionary wives became over-burdened, the RCA Board of Foreign Missions in 1869 appointed two young women, Martha T. Mandeville and Josephin Chapin, as assistant missionaries. Among others, Mrs. Sarah Scudder needed help in Chittoor, where she was engaged in leading a "female seminary" for Christian girls, some of whom would become suitable wives for evangelists and catechists. Mandeville and Chapin's role took a different turn, however, when within two years of their arrival they opened the Hindu Girls' School in Vellore. Contrary to the original plan for the mission, the school was designed to enroll upper-caste

Hindu girls who would carry their basic education and learning about the Christian faith into their Hindu homes without the expectation that their families would allow them to become Christians. While criticized by some missionaries and opposed by some men in the Hindu community, Hindu girls' schools were opened in other towns as well.

The success of the Hindu girls' school movement influenced a re-thinking of the Arcot Mission's decision not to open a variety of medical, educational, or other mission institutions. Low-caste people who converted to Christian faith suffered from great discrimination, deep poverty, lack of education and medical care, and limited opportunity for employment or land. In a caste-structured Indian society, Christians needed access to educational institutions, medical clinics and hospitals, and institutions aimed at economic development. By 1878, Arcot missionary statesman John H. Wyckoff recognized the wisdom of the Church of Scotland missionaries who were establishing colleges as well as high schools. Over the next several decades. high schools were opened in each of the major towns in the Arcot district, and Voorhees College was opened in Vellore.

Industrial institutes designed to promote economic uplift were opened, and unordained male and female missionaries arrived during the decades after 1880. Lambertus Hekhuis, William H. Farrar, and Bernard Rottschaefer developed an industrial school that taught carpentry and other crafts, and they developed a business model that eventually even ran a car dealership for a short time. The Women's Industrial Institute in Palmanair, under the leadership of Wilhelmina Jongewaarde, taught sewing and home arts to girls and young women and developed a marketing plan to assist its graduates to sell their products in India and elsewhere.

In spite of the great demand for medical healing, the Arcot Mission in 1854 reported that, since the colonial government had opened a medical dispensary in Arcot, the mission felt free to close its dispensary, sell its medical instruments, and use the balance of 87 rupees and 7 annas for literature in the Book and Tract Fund. However, the mission soon learned that it is not possible to isolate the preaching of the gospel from the urgent health needs of poor and out-castes. The mission re-opened the dispensary almost immediately and never ceased to respond to the wounded and sick who came to its doors by founding clinics and hospitals.

The situation today in the Arcot area

The present situation must be understood in light of the original policy of the mission: missionaries should focus on bringing individuals to faith and planting self-governing, self-supporting, self-propagating churches. When such churches come into existence, missionaries should consider themselves free to leave to serve in "regions beyond." The Arcot Mission took steps to implement that policy on the same day in 1853 when it established the Classis of Arcot as well as the Arcot Mission. That action meant that by the beginning of 1854 there was already a self-governing church in the Arcot district that functioned as an equal classis with all other classes in the Reformed Church in America.

In the beginning, the Indian church did not have sufficient strength to be self-supporting and self-propagating. It took decades to reach those goals. One major step toward those goals took place in Vellore in 1901, when churches related to the Arcot Mission joined together with churches related to the Free Church Mission of Scotland to form the South India United Church (SIUC). That resulted in a wider union when churches related to the congregationalist London Missionary Society and the Madura Mission, the Presbyterian Church of Scotland mission, joined together in the South India United Church in 1908 When the new church order of the South India United Church came into effect, the Classis of Arcot was transferred into that united church and its ecclesiastical existence in the Reformed Church in America came to an end, in fulfillment of the goal foreseen already in 1853.

The present situation is the result of the much wider union that took place in 1947 when the Church of South India was formed. It united the South India United Church with churches related to the Church of England, the English Methodist Missionary Society, and the Basel Mission. The Church of South India is the fulfillment of the hopes of early missionaries who looked for the day when an Indian church would be present to render the old mission agency structures outmoded.

The establishment of the South India United Church was the result of the desire of Indian Christians to overcome the denominational divisions of Europe and North America. It encouraged the old mission agencies to work more closely together in evangelism, to nurture congregations, to give attention to the needs of the economically and socially depressed in the churches, and to make a Christian contribution to Indian society. Missionaries and Indians associated with the SIUC

Dr. Ida Scudder with medical students in India

saw the need for strong Christian educational and medical institutions. The RCA cooperated in the Madras Presidency to establish high-quality union institutions, including Madras Christian Men's College, Madras Christian Women's College, St. Christopher's Women Teacher Training College, Voorhees College in Vellore, and Tamil-language men's' teacher-training schools. The Christian Medical Hospital and College, founded by Dr. Ida Scudder in 1918, became a leading Christian medical institution for the nation, with the international support of more than sixty churches and mission agencies.

Following the inauguration of the Church of South India in 1947, the congregations in the Telugu-language area were fully integrated into the Diocese of Rayalaseema, while those in the Tamil area were included in the Diocese of Madras. Assignment of missionaries to their places of ministry became the responsibility of the diocese rather than of the Arcot Mission or the RCA mission board. By the time the generation of missionaries appointed before World War II retired during the 1950s, Indians occupied the leadership positions in almost all of the institutions. By 1970, there were no ordained RCA missionaries serving in India.

The Diocese of Madras grew in numbers to the extent that in 1976 it was decided to create from it a new Diocese of Vellore that included most of the area formerly occupied by the old Arcot Mission. The first bishop in the new diocese was the Indian pastor, the Rev. Henry Lazarus. He moved forward in the spirit of Dr. John Scudder by giving priority to the task of evangelism and outreach, saying that the church existed for those outside it. He was succeeded by the Indian pastor Sam Ponniah, who called upon members in the towns and villages to be active in inviting friends and relatives to come to faith in Christ. Under the leadership of its first two bishops from 1977 to 1986, the number of members of the church in the Diocese of Vellore almost doubled from 47,000 to 96,000.

By 1970, the Arcot Mission's original purpose had been fulfilled. The Reformed Church in America moved on to "regions beyond" in other countries and continents, building new partnerships in mission. Today, RCA Global Mission lists on its website a much wider number of mission partnerships than ever before, but it feels free to trust the church in India to carry on the mission there. The conclusion of old official working relationships does not mean the end of the bonds of affection between Christians in India and the RCA. As this is written, the Rev. J. P. Sundarajan, who grew up in the Arcot area, is the director of RCA Global Mission. Individual congregations take on specific mission projects to assist the church in India in bearing witness to the gospel and meeting the needs of people in the villages of India, now at a time when a son of the Church of South India leads the RCA's calling to participate in worldwide mission.

Editors' update:

Mary Geegh served as a Reformed Church in America missionary to India from 1924 to 1962. In 1957, while serving as principal of the Girls' High School in Madanapalle, she founded the Geegh Nursery School, where children aged one-and-a-half to six years of the lowest caste could receive meals and Christian education while their parents worked in the fields. After retiring, she wrote a booklet called *God Guides* with the intent that the proceeds would help to support a portion of the Geegh Nursery School budget each year. In 1998, the baton was passed to Linn Gann (Mary's great niece), an RCA mission partner, to carry on an expansion of her legacy and ministry work through Mission Partners India (MPI) in Vellore and Madanapalle in the former Arcot Mission region of the Reformed Church in America in South India. MPI empowers marginalized low-caste families in India to rise above poverty through education at both Geegh Nursery School and Hope English

Children leaving the Geegh Nursery School in India

School, empowerment programs such as Give-a-Cow and Banyan Tree Tailoring programs, and village gathering places where villagers have a place to worship God.

For further reading

Arcot Mission of the Reformed Church in America: Jubilee Commemoration, 1853–1903; Vellore, India, January 8th, 9th, 10th, 1905. London: Forgotten Books, 2017.

David, Immanuel, *Reformed Church in America Missionaries in South India, 1839–1938: and Analytical Research*, 184. Bangalore: Asian Trading Corporation, 1986.

Fassler, Barbara. "The Role of Women in the India Mission, 1819–1880." In *Piety and Patriotism*, edited by James W. Van Hoeven, 149–62. Grand Rapids, MI: Eerdmans, 1976.

Heideman, Eugene. *From Mission to Church: The Reformed Church in America Mission to India.* Grand Rapids, MI: Eerdmans, 2001.

CHAPTER 3

China—1842

Linda Walvoord de Velder

The beginning

In the early 1800s, missions of the Reformed Church in America throughout the Far East and India followed five principles: 1) open schools and teach reading; 2) translate the Bible into the native language; 3) preach the gospel based on "an accurate knowledge of the mind of the people"; 4) seek definite and personal conversions; and 5) create settled churches with elected, local elders, gradually prepare native pastors, and form a seminary—all in order to build a church body of congregations that could continue to grow over the long term.

Missionaries could enter China safely only after 1842, when Britain settled the First Opium War, defeating the forces of the Qing Dynasty. Embassies and a military presence could now protect foreigners who came to trade, visit, or evangelize. The island of Hong Kong became a colony of the British in 1842, and four mainland ports were then opened to foreign trade, in addition to old trade routes into Shanghai. One of the ports was Amoy (Xiamen), which gradually became the principal port for tea. The Rev. David Abeel, the first Reformed Church in America (RCA) missionary to go to China, arrived in Amoy in 1842.

Abeel, in company with a doctor, stayed two years, established a small mission and wrote careful journals. He toured in England and America as a promoter of foreign mission. Abeel was a graduate of New Brunswick Theological Seminary in New Brunswick, New Jersey, founded in 1784 and a significant center of missionary zeal in later decades. The next missionaries to arrive were the Rev. John Van Nest Talmage, also from New Brunswick, with his wife, Mary. He tracked the Amoy dialect in phonetics (sound symbols) and charted it using the roman alphabet. His book, *The ABCs of Amoy*, spelled out the difficult dialect in a roman alphabet, adding diacritical marks to each word for the seven tones that controlled the meaning of words. For example, the words *snake* and *money* are spelled and pronounced exactly the same except for a tone or pitch. This phonetic system with tonal marks allowed missionaries (as well as Chinese students) to sidestep the entire Chinese writing system, which has 20,000 written characters standing for words. This romanized writing system was the single most revolutionary change, allowing China a bridge to the Western world. The literacy rate in China (i.e. using their native writing system) before this was less than 2 percent. In addition to using the romanized system, the missionaries could also learn a basic set of about 1,000 Chinese characters that would allow them fluency in two years or less. Luckily, graduates of RCA seminaries had already studied Latin, Hebrew, and Greek, but nothing really prepared them for this dialect, one of four major dialects that prevail in large regions of China.

How and with whom the RCA first got involved

The Rev. Elihu Doty and his wife arrived in the 1840s, and he made a dictionary of the Amoy language, building upon Talmage's system. Meanwhile, they began teaching and preaching as soon as they understood and could speak in simple ways, while translating the Bible from English into the romanized Amoy dialect. By the late 1840s, schools taught children and adults, and the arduous task of translating the Bible could take place. They also translated beloved Protestant hymns, liturgical prayers, songs, and other readings and lessons. These missionaries and their wives did sustained work—Doty for 20 years and Talmage for 43 years. Alongside them, a few English Presbyterian and United Church of Christ missionaries came, and later some missionaries from the London Missionary Society (LMS) arrived as well. They built the first Protestant church in China at Amoy and began to train native Chinese preachers and teachers, as well as "Bible women," to teach memory verses and hymns, even if they could not yet read.

An important book was written to describe the Chinese "mindset" and culture. The Rev. John Livingston Nevius, born in New York of Reformed and Presbyterian roots, toured China's early missions and regions and wrote *China and the Chinese* (1867). This encyclopedic, seminal book, written for missionaries, was in use for decades at both New Brunswick Theological Seminary and Western Theological Seminary. I own the copy that belonged to Henry Post, postmaster and leading citizen of Holland, Michigan, and friend of the Phelps and Otte families. Nevius promoted the "three self" movement: churches should become self-propagating, self-supporting, and self-governing. The last point—self-governing—would be a prominent one among the growing band of missionaries who came to Amoy.

Outstations gradually developed, served by traveling missionaries on mountain roads and rivers into the interior. By 1863, there were six congregations at Amoy worshipping in churches built by the mission or in rented spaces, and four of these had native pastors whom the missionaries considered to be ready to be ordained. Talmage and others pressed for a classis to form at Amoy: a self-governing body that could itself ordain elders, deacons and pastors, and carry out discipline and other planning. But some RCA voices back home in Synod and on the Board of Foreign Missions objected. They wanted the words "Dutch" or "American"—or, for the English Presbyterians, their own names—to be given to the churches. Talmage wrote to General Synod in a passionate and well-reasoned letter that "We were not sent here to form the Dutch American Reformed Church of China, or the English Presbyterian Church at Amoy, but the Church of Christ in China." The Amoy missionaries had met in an ad hoc council which they tactfully termed "the Great Presbyterial and Classical Council at Amoy." However, the folks back home called this gathering a foolish "improvising," and they wanted namesakes. Finally, four other missionaries with Talmage signed a letter threatening to resign if the board insisted on its view. The missionaries in China gradually won the point. The Amoy body followed a Reformed polity with lay elected elders alongside both native and foreign pastors using powers locally, not from faraway authority. In this way, Talmage, Doty and others became early founders of the ecumenical association of congregations of the Church of Christ in China today.

61 missionaries from various denominations attended a
conference in Amoy, China around 1935.

The wives of the missionaries and some single women were
educated in American colleges or the equivalent, even before 1900. They
wrote hundreds of letters each year. In the Chinese culture, men and
women in schools, hospitals, and churches were often kept apart. So the
Amoy churches adapted and put up screens in the center aisle so that
women and children could not see the men and vice versa, while the
pastor stood at the center in the front. This was never done in America,
England, or the Netherlands, but it met the local needs and customs.
Women of high birth in China and the Far East often had their feet
bound, and Chinese women in general were used to being subservient.
Some early converts in China were wives in polygamous marriages.
American and English women made an impression on the Chinese
in a way that priests and male missionaries could not do. The women
who served at Amoy over the hundred years from 1842 to 1949 deserve
their own chapter drawn from their journals, letters, and essays. Most
missionary letters and writings in China were destroyed in the various
revolutions and changes of war. The major storehouse of missionary
writings lies in America. Mission historians have suggested that in 1914
on the Protestant mission field, men outnumbered women three-to-
one, but in Amoy the ratio was closer to one-to-one.

A photo taken around 1935 at a conference in Amoy shows sixty-
one missionaries, of whom thirty-six are women (some of these folks
were from the Presbyterian or LMS mission agencies). A list of RCA
missionaries who served more than twenty years at Amoy or nearby
between 1842 and 1970 includes at least the twelve following surnames
(usually meaning husband and wife): Doty, Talmage, Kip, Warnshuis,
Otte, Koeppe, Walvoord, Holkeboer, de Velder, Veenschoten, Esther,
Boot, and more.

The "Woodie" station wagon with Chinese doctors and nurses and
Rev. Walter deVelder with toddler son John

The missions at Amoy by the 1930s not only erected beautiful buildings but brought better boats, motorcycles, and even a "Woodie" station wagon that the de Velder family owned to bring medical services as well as the gospel to the interior areas. By the late 1940s, the Communists pushed them out, but they "bought" the handsome Woodie from Walter de Velder to use in their parades.

When Tena Holkeboer assumed the headship of a girls' school at Amoy, her high school had 250 students in classes across an entire curriculum, not just reading and Bible study. The missionaries were also noted for music. The island of Kulangsu was sometimes called "piano island" after Helen Kip brought the first piano. One cartoon of the era shows a missionary descending from the sky with a Bible in one hand and a piano in the other. Musical missionaries popularized most hymns found today in the hymnbooks of the Christian Church of China.

By the time Joe Esther and John Muilenberg came to the Amoy mission and toured the outstations in the late forties, they not only had motorcycles (quite an improvement on the sedan chair!), but they also brought up-to-date cameras, printed pictures, recordings, the unforgettable flannelgraphs of their day, and mimeograph machines for making newsletters, lessons, and flyers. Even a printing press was kept at Amoy in John Talmage's basement before his retirement in the 1890s. Fortunately, good cameras, including films, meant that a substantial photographic record exists by the 1940s in albums and in magazines of the time—today found in America or England, and much less so in the drawers or files of China itself, as oppression forced the destruction of many records and mementos.

Some of the RCA missionaries were deported in 1950 when the Communists defeated the Nationalists, but they regrouped to serve Amoy-speaking Chinese people in Manila, the Philippines; Hong Kong; and Taiwan. Efforts with Amoy-speaking Chinese people outside of mainland China grew from and depended on the foundation laid at Amoy before 1950. In more than seven cases, RCA families who had served at Amoy spanned two generations as their grown children returned to mission work, increasing the numbers of missionaries in the 1920s and 1930s.

A case study of an RCA medical missionary

In addition to linguistics, translation of the Bible and other materials, establishment of schools, and development of churches and church leaders, the Amoy missionaries debated whether and when to introduce a medical doctor at Amoy. An early hospital begun by the English Presbyterians in Amoy had failed for lack of support and staff. Should the RCA try again?

This question was answered in 1887 with the arrival of the first Reformed Church missionary doctor sent to Amoy, Dr. John Otte. He was a remarkable combination of physician, missionary, architectural engineer, and writer of fascinating letters and reports. His story is a good example of how RCA missionaries worked in China.[1]

Otte brought the most up-to-date medicine of his time to Amoy, coming from the University of Michigan Medical School, a recently upgraded, clinically based program with professors teaching the "cutting edge" in surgery. This school was chosen by the father of Charles Mayo (of the Mayo Clinic) as a top school in the country. Mayo and Otte graduated close together and had the same specialty—ophthalmology, or eyecare. Like the Mayos, Otte's surgical skills and hospitals would expand in a huge practice of surgery of his day. In Amoy, Otte established a rigorous course of study and was able to train twenty Chinese doctors. He also founded a school of nursing, an essential but difficult task. His operating rooms and equipment as well as his wards compared well to the best in America. His dreams were big. Yet his own beginnings were humble. His story of humble beginnings with a very fine education is typical of many of the RCA missionaries.

---

[1]   Linda Walvoord deVelder, John deVelder, and Judy Tanis Parr, "A Medical Pioneer," *News from Hope College* (August 2011): 12–13.

Born in Flushing, the Netherlands, in 1861, John Abraham Otte was the son of middle-class tradespeople who immigrated to Grand Rapids, Michigan, when he was eight. To support his family, his father was a baker, a tailor, and a road worker at times. His parents valued education, and they sent him to Hope College's preparatory school and then to the college.

At Hope, he sought out every science class available, encouraged by Philip Phelps, then the college's president, and Professor Charles Scott, who became Hope's second president. Chemistry was already required of every Hope sophomore at that time. Professor Scott was hired to teach "natural philosophy," the older name for the natural sciences. There were already several medical doctors on the Hope board and in their constituency.

Otte graduated from Hope in 1883 and from the University of Michigan medical school in 1886. Then he spent a year in Utrecht, the Netherlands, to study surgical and treatment techniques under one of the world's leading eye doctors. The knowledge of Dr. Joseph Lister's research regarding sterile conditions in the operating theater were starting to take hold but were still widely resisted or poorly practiced in medical schools of the time. By the time he went to China, Otte understood what "sterile" meant.

Because his father, poor as he was, was an avid reader, he knew the director of the huge, famous Dutch orphanage at Neerbosch. The senior Otte had volunteered to raise money for that orphanage in the U.S. While in Utrecht, the young doctor Otte developed a link to this orphan home with over 1,000 children. He volunteered to help with the treatment of children on weekends. Becoming at ease with the children, he overcame his shyness about his odd voice and his dislike of public speaking. One day, he gave a warm address to the whole school assembled in an auditorium that seated 1,200. He told them that he planned to build a hospital in Amoy for the sick children of China and asked them to help. One little girl gave him five pennies that her uncle had given her for her birthday. Otte was so touched that he kept the pennies on a watch fob as a memento. Other orphans gave what little they could.

Later, he could tap prospective donors in the Netherlands and the U.S. by telling them of these children's open hearts. Even Queen Wilhelmina of the Netherlands gave him money, and he was soon able to go to China and follow his dream. While he in Utrecht, a famous eye doctor, when told of Otte's missionary plans, replied, "I know one other young doctor just as crazy as you are." The two men became roommates and lifelong friends, and Otte thereafter always had substantial ties to donors in the Netherlands.

In 1887, Otte came back to America and married his college sweetheart, Frances Phelps, daughter of Hope president Philip Phelps Jr. They had met on campus during his freshman year, where he often stood about smoking a pipe (for effect—a habit he later gave up). Her family lived in a college hall overlooking the pine grove. She was one of the first two women graduates of Hope College. They married in upstate New York, honeymooned in Europe for two months, and then traveled to China. By this time, she knew she was pregnant. Slowly, Otte had accumulated $1,200 toward his hospital.

They journeyed together to Amoy only to meet a roadblock. In New York, he had been appointed to medical work "in Amoy," but to the Ottes' utter surprise, the Classis of Amoy, which had the final say, had moved his assignment sixty miles upriver to a mountainous village called Sio-khe, where building would be even more difficult. The leaders at Amoy feared that Western medicine would be rejected by the Chinese. Superstitions about doctors were common, one being that they cut people's eyes out to make mirrors. Peasants feared that a hospital was part of a plot by "foreign devils." If his project failed, the leaders at Amoy wanted it out of the limelight, lest its downfall hinder the mission. Fran stayed in Amoy, and he went off to Sio-Khe.

In Sio-khe, he built his first hospital and named it Neerbosch after the orphanage. He slowly won the favor of the local mandarin. Sio-khe was the birthplace of Lin Yutang, author of *From Pagan to Christian* and many other books about China. But on opening day, peasants surrounded the gates and threw stones. A big thunderstorm soon broke out, which convinced them the gods were telling them to let the doctor's work begin. Otte treated eighty-five patients on the first day, and he gave thanks to God that none of them died that day. After the birth of their first child, Frances joined him there, and they lived in a house Otte planned and built.

Two years later, having proved his merit, Otte was allowed to move to Amoy to design and build two hospitals, first the Hope Hospital for men, and then, a year or two later, the Wilhelmina Hospital for women, linked to the first. He oversaw all of the construction and did some of the carpentry himself. Otte's interest in architecture had led him to design several houses in Grand Rapids during college as well as several buildings in Amoy. To raise money for his hospital, he designed elaborate Victorian cemetery monuments for wealthy people for hefty fees.

In 1900, at the time of the Boxer Rebellion, Frances returned to the United States with their four children. Missionaries had been killed in the north. Even in Amoy, the turmoil was severe. Their oldest son, John, born in 1887, who had gone to Grand Rapids to attend an American school and live with his grandmother since the family's previous furlough, was very lonesome. Otte accepted that he would have to stay in Amoy alone, writing frequent, poignant letters to Frances and the children. Between 1900 and 1910, he went home on two furloughs, once for a year and once for six months after suffering a severe hand injury.

In 1910, he contracted the pneumonic plague from a Muslim patient who called him to come to the mainland. When the patient vomited on his hands, Otte knew what had happened and washed in every chemical he had, but he died eight days later. Other doctors found the plague bacilli in Otte's system under microscope, but the serum was not available. A memorial service for Otte was held in Grand Rapids on June 16, 1910, and his students in China erected a monument to his memory. More than 1,000 people attended his funeral in Amoy.

After Otte's death, the two hospitals could be maintained only sporadically. During World War II, both were damaged in the Japanese occupation. Though damaged by war, the hospitals Otte built on Gulangyu were rebuilt and used for medical purposes until 2005.

In 2008, a large, 10-foot marble statue of Otte was erected in front of a brand-new hospital in Jimei, near Xiamen, honoring him as its founder. As it was ready to be dedicated, officials sought an Otte family representative who could attend. My husband, John R. de Velder, Otte's grandson-by-marriage, and I went to Amoy. John was invited to help unveil the statue, and at first, he was asked to speak for five minutes. Then it was reduced to two minutes; a few days later, word came he was asked to submit his talk for censoring and approval, and finally the last word came: he could not speak at all from the podium. Censors feared that John, an American pastor who himself managed pastoral care in a big hospital, would either give a Christian message or would insult or criticize the government. Otte's work and identity were a sensitive subject. The only words engraved on the statue are "Dr. John Otte, Dutch-American doctor" and his dates (1861–1910). This leaves a lot unsaid.

The statue of John Otte in Jimei, China, dedicated in 2008.

There on the podium, in two long rows, sat about 40 Chinese dignitaries of the city, the hospital, and the government, along with one foreign face—John's. After all the speeches, music, and introductions of these officials, John and a director silently pulled away a huge canvas and unveiled the statue. This act was more dramatic than anything he could have said. After the ceremony, which was covered by newspapers and TV stations, reporters swarmed to John de Velder asking their key question, "Why did John Otte come to Amoy?"

To answer the question, John again told the story of the Dutch orphans who gave pennies for the sick children of China. This conveyed the spirit of Otte's story without an overt Christian message or criticism of the government. The next day, three papers in Xiamen all carried front-page stories and a photo of the statue, with headlines like "Dutch Orphan Pennies Founded Hospital #2."

Years earlier, John Talmage had worked so hard to erase "Dutch" or "American" or "English" labels from the missionaries' work. Now the Chinese officials were eager to add "Dutch" and "American" on the handsome statue, probably to attract foreigners to Xiamen to showcase a sophisticated past history in Western medicine. Patients today who come for care at Hospital Number Two are asked to choose between the traditional Chinese herbal medicine/acupuncture wing and the Western wing. The people of China in the future will choose what they wish to follow. In 2008, the question "Why did Otte come to China?" won the attention and curiosity of the press because there was no answer on the statue, and they noticed that John de Velder wasn't allowed to speak.

The situation today

How many American and English or other missionaries were ousted from China in the purges after 1911 and after 1949? Stephen Neill, a mission historian, says that after 1911, 5,462 Protestant missionaries were expelled from mainland China, including 1,652 wives.[2] In 1949, a large number of missionaries were expelled by the Communists. The sixty-one pictured at Amoy in 1935 includes personnel from a variety of denominational backgrounds and locations. After 1949, mainland Christians met in secret with their native leaders and the Bible for the next sixty years. But the stories from the Amoy mission can be echoed in the stories of Chinese Christians down through the years.

Editors' update

The RCA missionaries in Amoy, China, held their last meeting together in 1949, and by early 1951, the last Reformed Church missionaries had been forced out of the country. As Eugene Heideman states,

> Within five years this loss had been turned into an opportunity: in cooperation with churches in Hong Kong, Singapore, Taiwan and the Philippines, the old Amoy Mission was now dispersed into a much wider geographical area, with the churches aiding each other to meet the new challenges.[3]

Many of those missionaries continued to use their Chinese language skills to work with Chinese nationals who had fled Communist China to start a new life elsewhere. The early work of RCA missionaries in Hong Kong, Singapore, Taiwan, and the Philippines was with Chinese Christians who had migrated. The Rev. Joseph R. and Mrs. Marion Esther went from Amoy to the Philippines, where they served until 1975. They broadcast radio programs to the Chinese, taught Chinese boys and girls in Manila, and worked in the churches to help alleviate

---

[2]   Stephen Neill, *A History of Christian Missions* (Baltimore, MD: Penguin Books, 1990), 288.

[3]   Eugene Heideman, *A People in Mission: The Surprising Harvest* (New York: Reformed Church Press, 1980), 69.

the many cross-cultural misunderstandings that occurred between the Philippine and Chinese Christians. The goal of the missionaries to incorporate the Chinese Christians into the existing Philippine churches was never successfully achieved.

For further reading

Amoymagic.com/amoymission.html (a collection of photos, book summaries, and articles about the Reformed Church of America Mission in China).

Bell, Jame E. "The Amoy China Mission of the Reformed Church in America, 1937-1951." *Grand Valley Journal of History* 4, no. 2 (2017).

Boehme, Hannah. "Tena Holkeboer: God's Bridge to the Chinese." *Joint Archives Quarterly* 21, no. 4 (2012): 1-4.

The Christian Intelligencer. Available at the Joint Archives of Holland, Holland, Michigan.

DeJong, Gerald. *Reformed Church in China, 1842–1951.* Grand Rapids, MI: Eerdmans, 1992.

deVelder, Linda Walvoord, John deVelder and Judy Tanis Parr. "A Medical Pioneer." *News from Hope College* (August 2011): 12-13

Esther, Joseph. *This is the Way, Walk in It.* Self-published, 1977.

Heideman, Eugene. *A People of Mission: The Surprising Harvest.* New York: Reformed Church Press, 1980.

Neill, Stephen. *The Pelican History of the Church: Vol. 6, A History of Christian Missions.* Baltimore, MD: Penguin Books, 1990.

Talmage, John. "Annual Reports to the General Synod." *Minutes of the General Synod of the Reformed Church in America,* multiple years. Available at the Joint Archives of Holland, Holland, Michigan.

White, Chris. "'Aliens Ministering to Aliens': Reformed Church in America Missionaries among Chinese in the Philippines." *International Bulletin of Mission Research* 42, no. 3 (2018): 203-40.

CHAPTER 4

Japan - 1859[1]

By Gordon D. Laman

The Reformed Church mission to Japan began in 1859. At that time, there was not even one Japanese Christian, not even one English-speaking person who could speak, read, or write the unusually difficult Japanese language, and it had been impossible for Western people to even visit or enter the island nation of Japan for 220 years. That situation was related to the fact that the arrival of the pioneer Protestant missionaries in 1859 was not Japan's first encounter with Christianity.

Early missionary activity in Japan

Roman Catholic Jesuit missionaries had arrived there 310 years earlier in 1549, during the period when feudal Japan had just begun the process of becoming united into one nation, which took place by means of brutal civil war under three successive dictators. During the period from 1549 to 1639, early Roman Catholic missionaries

[1] The research, data, and information offered in this chapter is derived from Gordon Dale Laman, *Pioneers to Partners: The Reformed Church in America and Christian Mission with the Japanese* (Grand Rapids, MI: Eerdmans, 2012).

from Portugal gained the patronage of feudal lords and dictators and brought about amazing results in converts using trained Japanese lay workers to establish churches and other institutions, but they did not translate the Bible into Japanese or train Japanese clergy. The situation of this Roman Catholic mission changed when the dictators realized the connection between Roman Catholic missions and colonialism in other places.

The combination of the success of these European Catholic missionaries with some of their unwise actions soon led to their being seen by the rulers as too influential and a threat to the dictator's authority. Consequently, the Roman Catholic mission resulted in banishment of all missionaries, antagonism toward Christianity, large-scale martyrdom of Japanese Christians, the absolute prohibition of Christianity, and finally in a policy of national isolation for the next two and a half centuries. From 1639 on, any surviving Christians in hiding were sought out, persecuted, and killed, and Christianity was labelled as a threat to Japan and prohibited on penalty of death. Those ninety years of Roman Catholic mission thus ended in the annihilation of that Christian movement and had the effect of a kind of inoculation of the Japanese people against Christianity.

When the Protestant foreign missionary movement in the West gained momentum in the early nineteenth century, American Christians sought ways to evangelize unreached people such as the Japanese. But it was only after 1854, when the U.S.'s Commodore Matthew Perry and his Black Ships induced Japan to end its isolation policy, and after Townsend Harris negotiated a treaty for trade in 1858, that Americans were able to enter Japan at two ports that opened in 1859. The Reformed Church responded immediately to this opportunity, sending three of the first six Protestant missionaries to Japan that very year.

RCA missionaries come to Japan

The Reformed Church Board of Foreign Missions raised the funds to send three families, and they appointed uniquely prepared pioneer missionaries to Japan. Samuel R. Brown, forty-nine years old and an experienced teacher and Reformed Church minister who had earlier served as a missionary to China, heard of the new possibility and applied to become a missionary to Japan. Brown then recruited Guido F. Verbeck, a linguistically gifted Dutch immigrant engineer who had felt called to be a missionary and was about to graduate from Auburn Seminary. The RCA, with a holistic view of

The three RCA pioneer missionaries to Japan in 1859,
l. to r.: Verbeck, Brown and Simmons.

mission, decided to send not only those prepared for evangelism and educational ministry, but also a medical missionary. Duane B. Simmons, MD, was recruited to fill that role. These three men became our first three missionaries to Japan. Missionary wives, soon called "assistant missionaries," would also play an important role in the work, but at that time only the men were actually appointed by the Board of Foreign Missions. These three men and their families sailed from New York, a journey of almost six months, arriving in Japan in November of 1859.

However, while these three missionary families were allowed to enter and live in Japan and were permitted to practice their own religion, the strict prohibition of Christianity on penalty of death for Japanese people was still in effect. The missionaries, under strict surveillance, were not allowed to witness to the gospel or do any evangelistic work among the Japanese. Brown and Simmons settled in Kanagawa (between Tokyo and Yokohama), and Verbeck went to Nagasaki. Learning the Japanese language became their first priority.

During his earlier service as a missionary in China, Samuel Brown had learned Chinese, and this proved to be a great asset. Spoken Chinese and Japanese are completely different. However, in the sixth century, the Japanese had adapted the Chinese characters as a basis for written Japanese, and Brown's knowledge of Chinese therefore proved very helpful in learning Japanese and in preparing materials so other missionaries could learn the language. He also soon began working on translating the New Testament into Japanese. As it turned out, Dr. Simmons left the mission after only one year, but he remained in Japan to practice medicine, where Western medicine was quickly being adopted and practiced by the Japanese. Consequently, in contrast to other RCA mission fields, medical mission did not become a major part of RCA work in Japan. The resignation of Simmons, however, freed funds for recruiting and sending another missionary family to Japan.

While learning the language in Nagasaki, Guido Verbeck focused on building trust relationships and on teaching classes in Western learning with promising young Japanese men. As a result of a Japanese government coup in 1868, young leaders formed a new government at Tokyo. Several of the new officials were former students of Verbeck at Nagasaki, and they invited him to work for the new government. Since the Christian prohibition was still in effect and direct evangelistic work was forbidden, Verbeck accepted the offer, hoping to quietly influence the government to remove the restrictions against Christianity. So, after ten years in Nagasaki, Verbeck worked for the government in Tokyo for the next ten years, and his work behind the scenes did in fact eventually help change the situation. The ban was finally lifted in 1873, and open evangelism could begin. In 1879, Verbeck, a brilliant linguist, returned to full-time mission work.

Meanwhile, following the resignation of Dr. Simmons, James and Margaret Ballagh had arrived to join the mission in 1861. The Ballaghs joined the Browns in Kanagawa, but soon, amid social unrest and assassination of some foreigners, the two families had to move to Yokohama for their safety. James Ballagh had begun language study and was preparing for evangelistic work. The language teacher assigned to him by the Japanese government was a Buddhist named Yano Riuzan. Ballagh's gifts did not qualify him to translate the Bible into Japanese, but he was a dedicated evangelist at heart. After a while, Ballagh asked his language teacher to help him translate the Gospel of John into Japanese. Ballagh remarked that his goal was "more to translate the Gospel into him than for the use of others." In spite of the prohibition, Ballagh and the other missionaries all found ways to teach the Bible in secret to a few interested individuals and small groups. James Ballagh secretly baptized this language teacher—the man's deathbed request—in 1864. This was the first-ever Japanese Protestant baptism, five years after the arrival of the first Protestant missionaries, and Mr. Yano never knew another Japanese Christian. At risk of death, a few additional baptisms took place in secret in the late 1860s.

The first Japanese Protestant church was organized on March 10, 1872, under the leadership of the RCA's James Ballagh. Many of the nine young men baptized that day, as well as several other converts, felt called to ministry and soon began theological study. Samuel R. Brown, besides his diligent work translating the New Testament into Japanese, began the first formal theological education in Japan in 1872 with ten students. So we see that, in contrast to the earlier Jesuit missionaries, our pioneer missionaries focused not only on learning the language so that they themselves could evangelize, but also on translating the Bible into Japanese and on training the early converts to become evangelists, pastors, and leaders of the Japanese Protestant churches.

At the time the first Protestant church was organized in March of 1872 under Ballagh's leadership, surveillance had become less strict, and it seemed hopeful that the government's absolute prohibition of Christianity might finally be lifted. Other denominations were sending missionaries to Japan, and Samuel R. Brown, reflecting his earlier positive experience of ecumenical cooperation in China, showed his concern for Christian unity in Japan. In a letter to the mission board, he wrote, "Now, from the ingathering of converts from this land, it seems as if all who love the Lord Jesus must wish to see such a foundation laid as that the church here shall be one and undivided, the 'Church of Christ in Japan,' rather than a church here of one name, others of another, confusing the heathen by its divisions, and weakening the power of the church thereby."[2]

On September 28, 1872, just six months after the first church was organized, Brown initiated the gathering of a convention of all the Protestant missionaries then working in Japan and a few other interested parties at Yokohama. While the Episcopalians declined to come, forty-three people attended, including the first Japanese elder, Ogawa Yoshiyasu, already a lay preacher. Reformed, Presbyterian, Congregational, and Baptist missionaries took part. Among other issues, the convention resolved unanimously to partner with leaders among the early Japanese converts to form one united Japanese Protestant church, rather than forming confusing branches of Western denominations. As it turned out, only the eventual six Reformed and Presbyterian

---

[2]   William Elliot Griffis, *A Maker of the New Orient: Samuel Robbins Brown* (London: Revell, 1902), 243–44.

missions honored this pledge, and Congregational, Baptist, Lutheran, Methodist, and other denominations were established in Japan. However, under Brown's leadership, the Reformed Church helped birth and foster the Church of Christ in Japan, which became the strongest, most independent branch of the Protestant movement in Japan.

Primary ministries completed by RCA missionaries

There were very gifted men among the early Japanese converts, and men such as Uemura, Ibuka, Maki, and Oshikawa not only became partners with the missionaries in evangelism and church-planting but also became the leaders of the independent Japanese church that began to grow and establish more congregations. Several gifted Japanese pastors also began to work with the missionaries to complete the translation of the Bible. Under the leadership of Samuel R. Brown, who enlisted the assistance of several gifted Japanese pastors from among the early converts, the New Testament was completed and published in 1880, one month before Brown's death at age seventy.

The RCA's Guido Verbeck, working with leading Japanese biblical and literary scholars Matsuyama, Uemura, and Ibuka, played a key role in Old Testament translation. Verbeck's translation of the Psalms is still revered by Japanese Christians today. The Old Testament translation into Japanese was completed, and a high-quality translation of the whole Bible was first published in 1887, a task spanning twenty-eight years from the arrival of the first missionaries. Verbeck also participated in theological education, and he was so gifted as a preacher in Japanese that he was called upon by the Japanese to travel the country incessantly as an itinerant evangelist until his death in Japan in 1899 at the age of sixty-eight.

Other RCA missionaries had joined the Japan Mission in 1869. Among them was Miss Mary E. Kidder, who joined the missionaries at Yokohama. She was the first woman appointed as a missionary to Japan, and she established the first girls' school in Japan, Ferris Seminary, in Yokohama in 1871. Henry and Elizabeth Stout replaced Verbeck in Nagasaki in 1869 and developed the work of the Japan mission on the southern island of Kyushu. The first person baptized by Stout was Segawa Asashi in 1873, and Segawa immediately began studying with Stout to prepare for the ministry. Henry Stout organized the first congregation in western Japan, Nagasaki Church, in 1876, established mission schools for both boys and girls there, and in partnership with

"Five Missionaries to Japan!" Rev. Alexander and Helena Van Bronkhorst and children saw their first mission car in the 1920s as the fifth missionary in their family

his protégé Segawa developed a theological education program in Nagasaki to train evangelists for church-planting in western Japan.

Beginning in the mid-1870s, the Reformed Church expanded its missionary force of both evangelistic and educational missionaries. Evangelism, church-planting, and training for the ministry, as well as mission school education in partnership with Japanese Christians, have always been the priorities of the RCA's Japan Mission. Furthermore, cooperation with like-minded missionary colleagues was always the policy of our mission. Accordingly, from the beginning of RCA mission work in Japan, partnership with the Presbyterian missionaries was the norm. The small early classes of the Reformed and Presbyterian missionaries for boys and men were joined together, culminating in the joint formation of the Meiji Gakuin in Tokyo in 1883, a secondary and college-level school for male education.

The RCA mission continued to develop the mission schools not only in Tokyo (Meiji Gakuin) but also in Yokohama (Ferris Seminary for girls) and Nagasaki (Sturgis Seminary for girls and Steele Academy for boys) as a way to reach the populace through education. The mission also continued to partner with the Japanese church leaders in theological education. At the same time, much of the work of the mission remained focused on evangelism and church-planting in partnership with Japanese pastors.

In 1877, within five years of the organization of the first Protestant church, the missionaries ordained the first Japanese pastors, including Uemura Masahisa, who became the most prominent minister and theologian in the Japanese church for several decades. These Japanese men immediately exhibited an independent spirit and assumed leadership roles. The Japanese-missionary partnership ushered in a period of rapid growth, and new churches continued to be established throughout the country. However, changes in the Japanese mission context, such as the rise of the Japanese empire, a reinvigorated nationalism, and its ultimate progression to militaristic ultra-nationalism led to a renewed anti-Western, anti-Christian reaction faced by both the mission and the Japanese church, and rapid growth of the Japanese church stalled. Faithful Japanese Christians have continued to serve and witness amid a society persistently resistant to the gospel.

Over the years, the missionaries' role in the task of evangelizing and developing the Japanese church evolved by necessity. In the beginning, they were the pioneers, the decision-makers and planners, since they started with zero Japanese Christians. They gradually needed to relinquish some of their leadership role and adjust their relationships as they moved to becoming partners with the Japanese Christians in the monumental task of witnessing to the gospel and forming a self-governing, self-propagating, and self-supporting evangelical Japanese Christian church in an anti-Christian environment.

World War II brought about a forced interlude in missionary activity, when the mission board recalled all missionaries for their safety. The Japanese government instituted strict surveillance and oppression of the Japanese church as well as persecution of Christians. As the war approached, all missionaries were evacuated. However, Sara Couch, who had served in Nagasaki since 1892 and had retired in Japan in 1937 at seventy years of age, declined to return to America and, though retired, she continued her evangelistic ministry among children, youth and women in partnership with her Japanese colleague, Miss Tomegawa Jun. During the war, Miss Couch spent almost three years in an internment camp amid very severe deprivation. She eventually survived the U.S. fire-bombing and destruction of the camp, and when the war ended, she returned to devastated Nagasaki to resume her work. However, six months later she died of pneumonia there in February of 1946 at the age of seventy-nine.

Missionary Sara Couch (right) with her colleague,
Tomegawa Jun in the 1930s.

Of the ministry of this devoted missionary, Albertus Pieters relates, "One incident of that work lives on in my memory. One Sunday, I happened to be in that city [Nagasaki], and Miss Couch asked me to go with her to one of her little Sunday schools. As we approached the place, the children recognized her and began calling to each other, '*Isoide, isoide, Yaso ga kita.*' 'Hurry up, hurry up, Jesus has come!' Of course, I know that the children meant that the Christian teacher had come, but what they actually said was, 'Jesus has come,' and I thought to myself, they speak more wisely than they know. Where this dear missionary comes, it is true that Jesus has come." Sara Couch is just one example of the many Reformed Church missionaries who have spent their lives as faithful witnesses to Jesus Christ in a nation notoriously resistant to the gospel.

During World War II, the Japanese militarist government forced all the Christian churches to come under one umbrella organization in order to facilitate their surveillance of Christianity. All denominations were thus dissolved, and the new organization was called the Nihon Kirisuto Kyodan (literally translated, the Japan Christian Church

Organization). After World War II, the once-again free and independent Japanese church retained the name forced upon it by the government, Nihon Kirisuto Kyodan, often abbreviated to Kyodan. In English, it is now called the United Church of Christ in Japan. After the war, the Kyodan welcomed the restoration of the relationship with American missionaries.

There was a window of opportunity for all Protestants to make a unified witness to the nation of Japan, but many North American denominations' missions, instead of partnering with the unified Japanese Protestant church, focused on their denominational identity and reverted to again developing Western denominations in Japan. However, eight Protestant denominations in North America, including the Reformed Church in America as well as Presbyterian, Methodist, Congregational, Evangelical and Reformed, Evangelical and United Brethren, Disciples of Christ, and United Church of Canada churches, together formed the Interboard Committee for Christian Work in Japan. Its purpose was to partner with and work under the leadership of the independent Japanese church. Here once again, the Reformed Church showed leadership in affirming its long-held policy of partnering with other Christians in the task of reaching the world for Christ. Consequently, after World War II, the Reformed Church sent many missionaries to partner with Japanese Christians to serve in the work of evangelism, leadership training, and mission school education in Japan.

The situation today in Japan

Over the course of the 160 years since the arrival of the pioneers, the Reformed Church has appointed and sent a total of 188 missionaries to serve in Japan. Many of them spent most of their adult lives serving Christ and his church faithfully and often creatively in Japan in obedience to their callings. By way of illustration, I mention only a few: Albert Oltmans pioneered continuing education for isolated pastors and evangelists struggling in church-planting; Sara Couch served for 54 years in evangelism among women and children; Albertus Pieters was the first to use newspaper evangelism for a larger witness; Jennie Kuyper, principal of Ferris Girls' School, died in the devastating 1923 earthquake; and Henry V. S. Peeke and Willis Hoekje, among numerous others, spent forty years or more alongside Japanese colleagues in district evangelism. Our partnership with Japanese Christians continues. The three RCA missionary couples serving in Japan in 2020 assist in theological education, in church renewal and evangelism, and in training for youth and children's ministry.

Japan remains a secular, materialistic society, resistant to the gospel. Japanese Christians and the Japanese church continue to express a desire for non-Japanese partners in their extremely challenging task of witnessing and of building up the body of Christ in twenty-first-century Japan. They do not need paternalistic foreigners to tell them what to do or how to do it, but they consider having missionaries to work along with them a great blessing and encouragement. They seek and rejoice in missionaries who will struggle alongside them. The urgency of the invitation to become partners in mission with Japanese Christians among one of the largest unreached populations in the world remains. We continue to be, in the words of RCA missionary Eugene Booth in 1891, "called upon to develop more of the grace of patient perseverance."

For further reading

Drummond, Richard Henry. *A History of Christianity in Japan*. Grand Rapids, MI: Eerdmans, 1971.

Griffis, William Elliot. *A Maker of the New Orient: Samuel Robbins Brown*. London: Fleming H. Revell, 1902.

Griffis, William Elliot. *Verbeck of Japan: A Citizen of No Country*. New York: Fleming H. Revell, 1900.

Heideman, Eugene. *A People in Mission: The Surprising Harvest*. New York: Reformed Church Press, 1980.

Laman, Gordon Dale. *Pioneers to Partners: The Reformed Church in America and Christian Mission with the Japanese*. Grand Rapids, MI: Eerdmans, 2012.

Verbeck, Guido F. "History of Protestant Missions in Japan." *Proceedings of the Osaka Conference of Missionaries in Japan, 1883*. Yokohama: Meiklejohn, 1883.

CHAPTER 5

Arabian Mission—1889

John Hubers

Stories passed around in RCA missionary circles—a kind of informal oral history of the Arabian Mission—often attribute the origins of the Arabian Mission to regular meetings held in the 1880s at New Brunswick Theology Seminary by three mission-minded students: Samuel Zwemer, James Cantine, and Philip T. Phelps. According to this account, these three met in a weekly prayer and study circle with a commitment to enter into the most difficult field imaginable for missionary service. They settled on Arabia because their Old Testament professor, Dr. John G. Lansing convinced them that it was the best fit for their criteria.

In point of fact, it may have been less dramatic than this, as James Cantine's more mundane account suggests:

> More likely I would have been a missionary somewhere, at home or abroad, but the first definitive step in my case came through Dr. Lansing—in his classroom and in his home. With his inherited interest—his father was a pioneer worker in Syria and Egypt—and with his burning zeal for the evangelization of Moslems, any active display of missionary interest was sure to be drawn into his

orbit. Through his class in the study of Arabic, and later in a little weekly prayer meeting for divine guidance, it was gradually made known to the three of us—Zwemer of the Middle Class and Phelps and myself of the Senior—that it was God's will that we should offer ourselves for work in Arabia.

When the three students and Dr. Lansing made their appeal for this new mission venture to the denominational mission board, they received the disappointing news that a massive debt would not allow for financial support at that time. Undeterred, they tried a different approach—a more direct appeal for individual donations through the creation of what came to be known as the Arabian Mission Syndicate, which would serve as a temporary bridge to later denominational support. By the summer of 1889, enough funds had been raised to allow Cantine to launch the mission after being ordained as a missionary by his classis in Kingston, New York. "O That Ishmael might live before thee!" was both the text of the sermon Dr. Lansing preached at Cantine's ordination and the motto that would accompany these early pioneers to Arabia.

Early missionary activity in Arabia

Cantine went first in the fall of 1889 because Zwemer still had another year of seminary to complete and Phelps decided to stay home to care for his parents. Cantine's port of entry was Beirut. There, he continued the Arabic language studies he had begun in New Brunswick and waited for Zwemer to join him. Zwemer did so a year later. Together, they worked to develop a basic mastery of Arabic before setting out to establish a missionary presence in the Arabian Gulf, their ultimate goal.

In his comprehensive history of the Arabian Mission, Lewis Scudder III emphasized the role of what were called *colporteurs* (peddlers of religious books) in the successful establishment of a mission presence in the Arabian Gulf in its early days. Some were members of the indigenous churches of the region. Others were converts, including a Syrian named Kamil 'Abd-ul-Masih al Aytani, the man Scudder identifies as the "third pioneer of the Arabian Mission and its first, and perhaps its only genuine, martyr." Kamil traveled with Cantine and Zwemer in their early exploratory journeys through the Gulf. By the time he died under suspicious circumstances (possibly poisoned), the mission had established its first mission station in the southern Iraqi port city of Basra (1892).

James Cantine, Dr. John G. Lansing, seminary
professor, and Samuel Zwemer

Over the course of the next ten years, three other mission stations would be added to Basra along with a growing contingent of RCA missionaries in Bahrain, Oman, and Kuwait. In each case, the aim was to establish an effective gospel witness in a part of the world that was known for its strong resistance to evangelization. Two early historians of the Arabian mission, Alfred De Witt Mason and Frederick J. Barny, describe the purpose of their mission in these terms:

> The object of the Mission, in accordance of its original plan, is the evangelization of Arabia. Our effort should be exerted directly among and for Moslems, including the slave population; our main methods are preaching, Bible distribution, itinerating, medical work and school work. Our aim is to occupy the interior of Arabia from the coast as a base.

What Zwemer, Cantine and al Aytani pioneered would develop over the course of the next eighty years into a well-established institutional presence with schools, hospitals and Bible shops in Iraq, Bahrain, Oman, and Kuwait. In Bahrain, the medical and educational work was groundbreaking, including the establishment of the first hospital (1903) and first co-educational school (early 1900s) in the

Dr. C. Stanley G. Mylrea
in the ward of the Mason
Memorial Hospital,
Bahrain, circa 1907.

region. The ultimate aim of the mission—the establishment of an indigenous church—was less forthcoming, with only a smattering of converts, enough to form one indigenous church for a relatively short time in Muscat, Oman. And that was in unique circumstances, as most of these converts were former lepers attached to a leprosy clinic established by the mission. They were, in other words, outcastes in their own society, making it easier to overcome the strong communal barrier that makes it difficult for Arab Muslims to abandon their religious birth identity. Missionaries who have served in the Arabian Gulf through the years have long asserted the belief (with some good evidence) that there have been a large number of indigenous believers who have embraced the gospel internally while being reluctant to make a public confession of faith. But visible, baptized conversions have always been few.

RCA missionary activity in Arabia

Two noteworthy events in the twentieth century would have a significant impact on the way RCA missionaries approached their calling. The first is evident in the voluminous writings of Samuel Zwemer, whose ministry bridged the tumultuous years prior to and just after World Wars I and II. The first turning point, in fact, was World War I. Prior to that time, Protestant mission work—not only in Arabia, but throughout the Global South—was often approached with optimism buoyed by the conviction that Christianity and the civilization it was associated with (Western civilization) would gradually, if not immediately, supplant other religious systems, including Islam. Zwemer's early writings reflect a kind of militant triumphalism with an accompanying language of conquest. Typical of this is something

Zwemer wrote to his supervisor about the proposed construction of a hospital in Bahrain in October of 1900:

> Surely we may pray definitely for so desirable an adjunct to our military equipment in this war for the Truth. If we can secure and hold that "kopje" the enemy will never dislodge us from Eastern Arabia.[1]

This kind of language gives way to a much less polemical tone in Zwemer's writings starting around 1916 when World War I was exposing the dark side of "Christian" civilization. And that was the turning point: a massively destructive world war that threw into question the triumphalist optimism of nineteenth-century missions. John Mott, a long-serving director of the Student Volunteer Movement, of which Zwemer was a charter member, revealed the radical nature of this perceptual shift in stark terms in an address he gave in Kansas City in 1914. His plea was for the continued need for mission *despite* the corrupting influence of Western civilization:

> The situation is more urgent than ever because of the rapid spread of the corrupt influences of so-called Western civilization. The blush of shame has come to my cheeks as I have seen how these influences from North America and the British Isles and Germany, not to mention other countries, are eating like gangrene into the less highly organized peoples of the world.[2]

From evidence found in his books, articles and letters, Zwemer seemed to move from "polemic to a hint of dialogue" from this time on.[3] This was evidenced by his addressing Muslims as "brothers" and speaking with admiration for the work of the great medieval Islamic scholar Abu Hamid Muhammad ibn Muhammad at-Tus al-Gazali (al-Ghazali), whose writing on prayer, wrote Zwemer, "attains almost to the heights of St. Paul."[4] Zwemer's evangelical fervor never diminished, but his respect and even admiration for the followers of what he called "the greatest of non-Christian religions" grew as the years went on.

A revulsion at the violence of Western civilization was certainly

---

[1]   Samuel Zwemer to Dr. H. N. Cobb, October 6, 1900.

[2]   John Mott, qtd in John Hubers, "Samuel Zwemer and the Challenge of Islam: From Polemic to a Hint of Dialogue" *International Bulletin of Missionary Research* 28, no. 3 (2004): 119.

[3]   Hubers, "Samuel Zwemer and the Challenge of Islam."

[4]   Hubers, "Samuel Zwemer and the Challenge of Islam," 21.

one factor for this change of attitude. Another was a natural reaction to neighborly relationships developed in a culture celebrated for its hospitality. Zwemer and his missionary compatriots became close friends with their Muslim neighbors which made it more and more difficult to maintain the stereotypical caricatures either of Muslims as people or the faith that animated their lives.

This is illustrated by something Zwemer included in the commemorative volume he and Cantine wrote for the fiftieth anniversary of the Arabian Mission. Here, he spoke warmly about friendships he made with Bahraini neighbors. There is no doubt that this was also a factor, perhaps the prime factor, that inspired Zwemer's move from polemic to a hint of dialogue.

> Friendships begun that first year endured for decades. Hasan Musherif, the pearl merchant, was an example. He never became a Christian, but again and again he proved a friend in need and as defender against slander, a counselor of wisdom and man of pure heart and life. When our children were born he gave each of them a beautiful Arabic name. And when Katherine and Ruth died in the same week he was like a brother to us in our sorrow.[5]

Lyle Vander Werff identified this perceptual shift as a move towards a more "anthropological-Christocentric approach to Islam." It would become a definitive motif not only for Zwemer but for the Arabian Mission as a whole in the years to come, even when its official status ended in 1973. Vander Werff believed that this shift was liberating for Zwemer. I would suggest that it was true for many who would come after him, as well.

> It is almost as if Zwemer is a liberated man. No longer is it his duty to make battle against Islam as a system. He can now concentrate on the message which is Christocentric and eschatological, a message of Good News for the Muslim as a man (sic).[6]

The door was now open for a more dialogical approach to mission, even though Zwemer did not go as far in that direction as missionaries

5   Zwemer and Cantine, *The Golden Milestone*, 115.
6   Lyle L. VanderWerff, *Christian Mission to Muslims: The Record: Anglican and Reformed Approaches in India and the Near East, 1800–1938* (South Pasadena, CA: William Carey Library, 1977), 243.

Dr. Paul W. Harrison in traditional Arab
dress ready to cross the desert

do today. How far is evidenced in the current work of the Al Amana
Center in Oman, which operates in a cooperative relationship with
the Omani government to bring Muslims and Christians together for
dialogue around matters of common concern while still maintaining a
faithful gospel witness.

What is now the centerpiece of Al Amana's ministry as a further
development of Zwemer's shifting perceptions was on full display at an
extraordinary three-day missionary gathering that took place in Cyprus
at a mountaintop hotel resort in the fall of 1977. Representatives
and missionaries from all the European and American organizations
operating in the Arabian Gulf were present at this meeting, as were
heads of the various communions, including RCA general secretary
Arie Brower. Bible studies were led by the venerable Dr. Kenneth Cragg;
a keynote address was given by the General Secretary of the Middle East
Council of Churches; and panel discussions were led by the last of the
long-serving RCA missionaries working in Kuwait, Bahrain, and Oman.

My wife and I were present at this stimulating event, having just
spent a year as volunteer missionaries in Bahrain. What we learned at
this gathering helped us understand how far our missionaries had come
in developing respectful dialogical relationships with their Muslim

neighbors. One of the participants, Dr. Harold Vogelaar, defended this approach as fully in keeping with what the mission had always been about: bearing witness to the good news of Jesus Christ among our Muslim neighbors:

> I am pleased to observe that an ever-wider circle of Christians are taking [dialogue] seriously and commending it as a Christian way to approach people of other faiths. In his book, *Christian Mission in the Modern World*, John Stott ... commends dialogue because when engaged in sincerely, it bears the marks of authenticity, of humility, of integrity and of sensitivity. ... Through true dialogue the Gospel is not compromised nor its message subjected to syncretism; on the contrary, its truth is more clearly illumined and sincerely appreciated.[7]

Primary ministries completed by RCA missionaries

In the fall of 1971, an East African church leader named John Gatu visited general assemblies of various Reformed bodies in the U.S., including a major RCA mission conference. His message was controversial and not well received in many quarters. But the RCA took it to heart, at least in the larger concern it addressed. Put in its starkest terms, what Gatu was calling for was a moratorium on missions, particularly in Africa. "Missionary, go home," he said. The issue, according to Gatu, was an unhealthy dependency that had stunted the growth of Christianity in the continent as well as other parts of the world, where missionaries continued to cling to dominant supervisory roles.[8]

While the RCA did not withdraw missionaries from their places of service in response to Gatu's challenge (which other East African church leaders thought to be too extreme), they were attuned to the concerns it raised. A policy of de-institutionalization, which had begun earlier in India, continued apace in the early 70s. No longer would the RCA run hospitals and schools and other institutions as property owners and supervisors. In each of our various locations around the world, mission properties were either sold or given to indigenous Christian organizations and denominations.

[7]   Harold Vogelaar, unpublished transcript, 1977.
[8]   The RCA denominational magazine, *The Church Herald*, was, interestingly, the only publication that reproduced this address verbatim. See the November 5, 1972, edition.

It was at this time—the early 70s—that this policy took hold in the Gulf. But it was more problematic there than elsewhere because there was no indigenous church to which the institutions could be relinquished. In this case, it was determined that the hospitals should be sold to the respective governments.[9] The hospitals in Oman were sold to the Omani government for a token 1 riyal (the equivalent of $2.50), while the hospital in Kuwait brought in enough revenue to provide a hefty financial cushion for global mission in general for a number of years. The bookstores, now a chain called The Family Bookstore, would be operated by the Middle East Council of Churches, and the schools would be put under the supervisory control of Arabic-speaking congregations. The first mission station in the region, Basra, Iraq, had already relinquished its hold on mission institutions, although in that case it was not voluntary, as the Baathist revolution that overthrew British colonial rule in the 1960s also turned against a Western missionary presence. Our missionaries were forced to flee the country as the government took possession of the hospitals and schools they had been operating.

This de-institutionalization signaled a new working relationship that made the career missionaries feel at times as though the earth had shifted beneath their feet. What it meant practically was that the Arabian Mission no longer existed as a policy-making body. And that was a difficult shift for those who had spent their adult lives cocooned in its institutional embrace. Lew Scudder alludes to the distress it caused when missionaries were trying to deal with the other new reality of the Gulf in the 1960s and 70s: the burgeoning presence of a large expatriate population among whom were thousands of Christians needing spiritual nurture. It was hard to figure out how ministering to expatriate Christians fit into the initial purpose of the Arabian mission. The fragmentation that was a result of the effective dissolution of the Arabian Mission caused a consternation that was never fully resolved among the long term missionaries.

In the Arabian Mission's experience an ambiguity arose. It was probably inevitable that it should. To all intents and purposes, for over a half century the Arabian Mission as a community— missionaries and "native helpers" alike—formed the core of the Church in the Gulf. Apart from a few British civil servants,

[9]   With the notable exception of the American Mission Hospital in Bahrain, whose ruler insisted that it maintain its existence as a mission institution.

journeymen diplomats, tradesmen, shopkeepers, an explorer or two, and the odd semi-itinerant businessman, they were all there was of the Church. They met all together for worship, and more often than not it was with those civil servants, diplomats and tradesmen that they built, operated and served as mission-church. But it was commonly acknowledged that not only was the root identity of the church missionary, but the mission was also distinctly "American." It was known by all as the American mission. In that commonly acknowledged identity were seeds of ambiguity.[10]

The situation today in Arabia

Once the Arabian Mission was disbanded, the mission lost much of its sense of common purpose. Previous generations of missionaries had gone through stringent training in language-learning and cultural orientation to prepare for and live up to a communally determined missional vision. Now their purpose and preparation were determined primarily by the demands of the institutions that hired them. Pre-departure or even on-site cultural orientation became more difficult, as new hires had to be on site almost immediately when positions came open. Language training was another casualty of de-institutionalization, as it became difficult to manage for all save the fortunate few who were able to pick up languages more easily.

Another factor that would alter the impact of an RCA mission presence in the Gulf was the reduced number of positions available for missionaries to fill. Fewer institutions meant fewer jobs. The only positions occupied by RCA missionaries at that time were pastors for international congregations in Bahrain and Oman, the chief medical officer and chaplain of the American Mission Hospital in Bahrain, the principal of Al Raja School in Bahrain, and the two directors of the Al Amana Center in Muscat. And in all these cases they would work not for the RCA, but for the institutions that hired them. Yet even as the missionary presence was reduced, so the number of expatriate Christians expanded and provided a larger base for Christian witness. That is one reason why the RCA provides pastors for the expatriate congregations in several countries. A prime calling of the ministry in these congregations is to equip the saints for their missional outreach. The gospel witness has not been reduced. It has simply taken on a different shape.

[10] Scudder, *The Arabian Mission's Story*, 421.

A shift to a less institutional footprint for mission is not unique to the Gulf. It is the story of mission around the globe, a return to a tent-making model of ministry that operates out of a position of relative weakness, relinquishing an earlier control that was fraught with difficulties, not least of which was the dependency that John Gatu decried. This is our new reality. Given the growth and vitality of the church in Africa, Asia and Latin America, missionaries now work in a collaborative way with their national partners. What this means for the future of a gospel witness in the Arabian Gulf, where there is no indigenous church, is yet to be determined. The years of well-developed relationships, framed in the context of a faithful, Christ-like presence through the ministry of the Gulf expatriate churches today, means that Christian witness with its God-determined impact will continue. We know it will. God promises it will:

> As the rain and the snow
>   come down from heaven,
> and do not return to it
>   without watering the earth
> and making it bud and flourish,
>   so that it yields seed for the sower and bread for the eater,
> so is my word that goes out from my mouth:
>   It will not return to me empty,
> but will accomplish what I desire
>   and achieve the purpose for which I sent it. (Isaiah 55:10, NIV)

For further reading

Armerding, Paul L. *Doctors for the Kingdom: The work of the American Mission Hospitals in the Kingdom of Saudi Arabia.* Grand Rapids, MI: Eerdmans, 2003.

Boersma, Jeanette. *Grace in the Gulf.* Grand Rapids, MI: Eerdmans, 1991.

Heideman, Eugene. *A People in Mission: The Surprising Harvest.* New York: The Reformed Church Press, 1980.

Heusinkveld, Paul. *Elephant Baseball: A Missionary Kid's Tale.* Grand Rapids, MI: Eerdmans, 2017.

Hubers, John. "Samuel Zwemer and the Challenge of Islam: From Polemic to a Hint of Dialogue." *International Bulletin of Missionary*

Research 28, no. 3 (2004): 117–21.

Luidens, Donald A. *Seeds of Hope, Seeds of Hate: A Love Story (Begins)*. Holland, MI: Van Raalte Press, 2016.

Mason, Alfred De Witt and Frederick J. Barny. *History of the Arabian Mission*. New York: Reformed Church in America Board of Foreign Missions, 1926.

Scudder, Lewis R., III. *The Arabian Mission's Story: In Search of Abraham's Other Son*, Grand Rapids, MI: Eerdmans, 1998.

Transcripts and papers from the Cyprus Conference (1977) in possession of the author and the RCA Archives in New Brunswick, New Jersey.

VanderWerff, Lyle L. *Christian Mission to Muslims: The Record: Anglican and Reformed Approaches in India and the Near East, 1800–1938*. South Pasadena, CA: William Carey Library, 1977.

Van Ess, Dorothy F. *Pioneers in the Arab World*. Grand Rapids, MI: Eerdmans, 1974.

Zwemer, S. M. and James Cantine. *The Golden Milestone Reminiscences of Pioneer Days Fifty Years Ago in Arabia*. New York: Fleming H. Revell Company, 1938.

CHAPTER 6

RCA Mission Work Among Native Americans—1895[1]

LeRoy Koopman and Bill DeBoer

Beginnings

The RCA began reaching out to Native Americans soon after the Dutch first settled in New Amsterdam. It was in the late 1600s that pastors from the Albany and Schenectady churches began to preach to them. There was some success, as there are records of converts being baptized and received as members in these and other churches in upstate New York. These mission efforts waned due to several factors: hostility between the Native Americans and settlers due to White encroachment on Native lands, failure to organize distinctively Native congregations that reflected their cultures, and a lack of pastors who made Native American evangelism a priority. The Revolutionary War effectively put an end to this mission work, and it would be 130 years before the RCA began reaching out to Native American peoples again, and this

---

[1] The research, data and information offered in this chapter is derived from LeRoy Koopman, *Taking the Jesus Road: The Ministry of the Reformed Church in America Among Native Americans* (Grand Rapids, MI: Eerdmans, 2005).

would be much farther west. Mission activities were later initiated in six distinct geographical locations, each of which has its unique story.

Mission to Native Americans in Oklahoma

In the late 1880s, the mission work of the RCA was conducted by the Board of Foreign Missions and the Board of Domestic Missions, both of which were led by men. Supplementing the work of the domestic board was the Women's Board of Domestic Missions, whose duty it was to provide funds for building and furnishing parsonages in the Midwest.

The women's board eventually became bored with buying couches and curtains for parsonages and began to explore other areas of ministry. At that time, the country was preparing for the 1893 World's Fair in Chicago, called the "Columbian Exposition" in commemoration of the 400th anniversary of Christopher Columbus's arrival in the Americas. The board hit on the idea of establishing a "Columbian Memorial" for Native American mission, since, while the arrival of Columbus had caused great distress for the Native peoples, it also placed them in a position to hear the gospel.

But how would the women raise money to launch this new venture? They sponsored a mission tea at the Reformed Church headquarters in New York City. The tea produced gifts totaling $3,093.96—at a time when bread was selling for 3 cents a loaf.

A search for someone to carry on this new work led them to the New York sickbed of Frank Hall Wright, an itinerant evangelist who was the son of a Choctaw minister and a White missionary teacher. Despite his serious illness of tuberculosis, Wright accepted the challenge.

In May of 1895, after dropping off his wife and children with family in Dallas, Texas, Wright procured camping equipment and a helper and set out for Native American territory. He went, as agreed, to the Fort Sill military installation adjacent to Lawton, Oklahoma. There he had determined to bring his message to Geronimo's band of Chiricahua Apaches, who had been held there as prisoners of war since 1886. He also intended to reach the Comanches, who had voluntarily established a camp near the fort.

But Wright was turned away by both the government and the Native Americans. He then heard of a settlement of Cheyennes and Arapahos at Colony, Oklahoma, 150 miles to the north. Still wishing to fulfill his mandate, he made the journey and found there a government agency and school directed by John Seger, a devout Christian. Seger invited Wright to preach to the children on a Sunday morning, and, impressed by his earnestness and eloquence, urged him to stay and establish a mission there. The board agreed, and the Columbian Mission of the Women's Board of Domestic Missions was established.

Wright spent time with his family each winter in Dallas, and while there became acquainted with the Rev. Walter Roe, a Presbyterian pastor, and his wife, Mary. Wright, more inclined to itinerant evangelism, challenged Roe to partner with him as pastor of the church in Colony while he continued to make evangelistic tours in the surrounding territory.

Roe readily accepted and quickly became the inspirational and guiding force of the RCA's Native American ministry. The church at Colony closed in 1932 as a mission of the Reformed Church after most of the Native Americans moved elsewhere. But for some thirty years, the "Columbian Mission" played the role of the mother church to the RCA's emerging Native American congregations.

Among the practices and policies that Roe introduced to the ministry were

1. "Open" parsonages, a sign of social acceptance and an opportunity for informal witness.
2. Community centers called lodges: gathering places that included stoves, washtubs, medical treatment rooms, easy chairs, books, games, and recreational equipment.
3. A full range of church activities, including morning and evening worship services, Sunday schools, sewing clubs, Christian Endeavors, and choirs.
4. An annual "giving Sunday," designed to teach stewardship of time and talents in addition to gifts.
5. Camp meetings, the Christian answer to pow-wows and the highlight of the church year. Native Americans from many tribes gathered for four days under a huge tent for feasting, socializing, and preaching. Pastors and guest speakers invited listeners to "take the Jesus road," while interpreters simultaneously translated the message for Native Americans gathered in various language groups. It was at a camp meeting that Geronimo later announced his decision to adopt the Christian religion.

The Apache Mission and Church

Roe and Wright eventually received permission to establish a Christian mission, including a school for the Apache children. (The Comanches already had a government school.) The school was ready in the fall of 1899, and two unmarried women, F. A. Mosely and Maud Adkisson, joined the mission team. They were the first of scores of teachers, housemothers, nurses, traveling visitors, and Bible teachers who over the years were the unsung heroes of the RCA's mission effort. The Apache mission school and worship services flourished, and several of the tribe's leaders, including Christian Naiche, its hereditary chief, urged their people to "take the Jesus road."

In March of 1905, President Theodore Roosevelt's inaugural parade included the Apache warrior Geronimo, riding his horse. Roosevelt said to a reporter, "I wanted to give the crowd a good show." Both Roosevelt and Geronimo were members of the Reformed Church in America. Meanwhile, work among the Comanches was producing results, and the Apache church and the Comanche church were organized on May 1, 1907, with the Apaches meeting in the morning and the Comanches in the afternoon.

The Apaches had been held as prisoners of war near Fort Sill, Oklahoma, since 1894. Finally, after 19years, they were assigned to join the Mescalero Apaches on their reservation in New Mexico. Most accepted the offer, but some opted to remain in Oklahoma and became the nucleus of the Apache Reformed Church in the nearby town of Apache. For several years, the Apache church relied on lay leadership, including long-time tribal chairperson Mildred Cleghorn. The Apache church received its first full-time pastor when lay people Andy and Marjorie Kamphuis arrived. They came in 1962 and stayed for twenty-three years. Other missionary couples followed to give leadership to the church.

The Apache Reformed Church has now been without an ordained pastor for almost a decade, but the church members, including those preparing to become commissioned pastors, continue to provide necessary leadership.

The Comanche Mission and Church in Oklahoma

The first Comanche convert was a teenager, Dorothy, who played a personal role in the conversion of her uncle Nahwats, a leading medicine man. Tragically, Dorothy died at the age of sixteen, but her influence extended far beyond her lifetime as her entire family became pillars of the church. Her younger brother, Robert Chaat (the original family name was Chahtinnaecekque), was ordained in 1934 as the RCA's first Native American pastor and served his home church in various capacities for forty years.

After sharing missionaries with the Apaches for several years, several Comanche leaders requested a church building and a pastor of their own. The result was the arrival of pastor L. L. Legters and the construction of a small building painted bright yellow, referred to as the "yellow mission." That church was replaced in 1941 by an attractive building incorporating several shades of brown and tan stone from a nearby quarry.

From the beginning .the Comanche church has been the most self-supporting of all the RCA Native American congregations, aided in part by a substantial gift of "oil money" left by one of its members. In 1962, the church moved beyond mission status to become self-supporting. Even with continuing budget constraints, the congregation's lay people still take responsibility for all the ministries, including preaching, teaching, youth work, and an effective healing ministry.

The Mescalero Mission and Church in New Mexico

In 1913, a special train with 170 former prisoners of war from Fort Sill, 87 of whom carried transfers of church membership, arrived at Mescalero, New Mexico. There they joined a mission that had already been established by the Reformed Church with E. B. Fincher, a Southern Presbyterian, as the missionary.

The Mescaleros and the Fort Sill Apaches got along reasonably well, and the work flourished. Mission centers were established at the outlying settlements of White Tail, Carizzo, and Elk Silver, in addition to Mescalero, and every Sunday mission workers traveled more than a hundred miles over winding roads to teach and conduct worship services. Among the church leaders was Dorcie Kazhe, who taught Sunday school for fifty-nine years and spoke throughout the denomination on behalf of Native American mission. One son of the church, Wendell Chino, served for four years as pastor of the church but is best known for his four decades as a tribal leader and for his outspoken defense of Native American rights on the national level.

The ministry at Mescalero has been blessed with several long-term and respected pastoral couples. A new church building was dedicated in 1949, and an addition was added in 1998. Mescalero Reformed Church

Vacation Bible Schools teachers at the Jicarilla Apache
Reformed Church in Dulce, New Mexico

continues to be a strong congregation that is deeply involved in all
aspects of community life.

The Dulce Mission and Church in New Mexico

A second mission in New Mexico was founded in 1914 on the
Jicarilla (pronounced "hick-a-REE-ya) Apache reservation centered in
the town of Dulce in northern New Mexico near the Colorado border.

It was Walter Roe who discovered the critical needs of the Jicarilla
people and urged the Women's Board to begin a ministry there. The
board responded by sending a Presbyterian layperson, Denton Simms,
and community worker Hendrina Hospers, who stayed thirty-two
years. In 1918, the government school in Dulce was transformed into a
clinic for victims of tuberculosis and influenza. The mission responded
by building a school and dormitories. Church and Sunday school
attendance was required, as it was for all mission schools.

In 1924, ten years after Simms arrived, the church was organized
with 57 members, both Native American and White. In 1935, the
government took back the school, but the mission retained the
dormitories and was able to provide a strong witness through the many
housemothers who served over the years.

The Winnebago Reformed Church in 1997

Like the Mescalero church, the Dulce church has been served over the years by many exceptional pastoral couples. The church has been a steady presence in the community since its beginning, and that remains true today. Since Brad and Robin Kautz arrived in 2013, membership is up slightly and many unchurched people in the community come during times of crisis in their lives, as the church continues to be recognized as a stabilizing force in the community.

The Winnebago Mission and Church in Nebraska

By the early 1900s, the Reformed Church had founded two non-reservation missions in Oklahoma (Apache and Comanche) and two reservation missions in New Mexico (Mescalero and Dulce). Later, the RCA assumed responsibility for two additional reservation missions, this time in northeast Nebraska. The Presbyterians had established mission work there among the Winnebagos at Winnebago and the Omahas at Macy. But the work had faltered, and the RCA, noting the proximity to the Reformed churches in northwest Iowa, took over the Winnebago work in 1908 and the Macy work in 1934.

The RCA opened a mission boarding school at Winnebago in 1917, and education and child care became a priority of the Winnebago mission. When the school closed in 1928 because of the availability of public education, the mission continued to provide dormitories and housemothers. Over the years, the dormitories morphed into youth shelters, followed by group homes, foster care, and day care. A key person in all of these phases of ministry was Bernice Tegeler of Erie, Illinois, who served more than fifty years at Winnebago.

Since then, worship attendance has grown, but finding leadership for the congregation has been a challenge, as is finding adequate funding, since RCA Global Mission ended its support in Winnebago in 2005. After eleven years in ministry, Lowell TenClay and his wife Connie are retiring, and their number-one priority is preparing the congregation to provide the leadership of the various facets of the church's ministry.

The Macy Mission and Church in Nebraska

The RCA's ministry among the Omaha people in Macy has arguably been the most challenging of all of the Native American mission efforts. The Omaha reservation was—and is—one of the most economically and socially depressed Native American communities in America.

The first RCA pastor in Macy was the Rev. George Laug, a former missionary to Japan. Within a few years, the white clapboard church had been moved near the powwow grounds. Sunday schools were being conducted at two locations, and vacation Bible schools were being conducted at three locations.

A new church building was dedicated in 1943, but attendance was minimal, and early RCA missionaries voiced concern about the inroads of various sects and the use of peyote as a religious sacrament. Nevertheless, several pastors and Omaha lay leader Thurman ("Happy") Cook have over the years provided a faithful and steady Christian witness to the tribe. Unfortunately, this struggling church was closed in 2009.

An era of Native American pastors

From the earliest days of mission to the Native Americans west of the Mississippi, the Reformed Church has provided mission schools and boarding schools as a vital element in their ministry. As some of the young people emerged as potential leaders, the RCA provided financial and staff support for the Cook Christian Training School in Phoenix (and later, Tempe), Arizona, a school specifically designed to prepare Native Americans for Christian service.

Over the years, and especially during the 1950s and 1960s, seven Native American pastors were ordained to the gospel ministry. Of these, four studied at the Cook school in Arizona and four graduated from theological seminaries. Robert Chaat, Comanche, served over forty years as assistant, pastor, and moderator of the Comanche Reformed Church. James Ottipoby, Comanche, was assistant at Winnebago and Mescalero and later a military chaplain. Wendell Chino, Mescalero Apache, served as assistant and pastor at Mescalero and then as tribal chairperson for forty-three years. Wilbur DeCora, Winnebago, was the pastor at Mescalero and Winnebago. Jonah Washington, Pima, pastored the churches at Mescalero, Apache, and Dulce, then became part of the staff of the Chilocco (Oklahoma) Native American school. Frank Love, Omaha, was pastor at Mescalero and Macy and then became employed by several Native American services and agencies. Earl Smith, Oneida, served as pastor at Macy.

Recent ministry initiatives

Urban Native American ministry has been a main thrust of the Center of Hope in Sioux Falls, South Dakota, since its beginning in 2000. Although this is not an exclusively RCA mission, it was founded by RCA pastor Fred Wilgenburg and is partially funded by RCA Global Mission. Right from the beginning, the neighborhood surrounding the center had a high population of Native American people. While the recipients of ministry are not exclusively Native, Native people make up 44 percent of the people served.

The center carries out its mission by having multiple ministries:

- A Care Center with computers, phone, work clothes, pastoral care, and winter clothing. This is a resource center of the city of Sioux Falls and has two pastors to visit with people.
- Faith Community Nursing: on staff are two part-time nurses who help guests and work with three universities in training new nurses in clinical skills. The nurses also advocate for patients with their doctors.
- A mother/baby basket component for new mothers with basic health information, diapers, and clothing.
- A fully operational bike ministry that rebuilds bicycles for people who have lost driving privileges. This helps them get to work. The bicycles are utilized year-round.

All these activities often lead to spiritual conversations. The most effective person in Native ministry at the center is Brian Narcomey, a Native American from the Comanche Reformed Church.

Ministry at Calling Lake, Alberta, Canada

In 1998, twelve members of the Athabasca Reformed Community (RCA) in Alberta, Canada, drove thirty miles every other Sunday to the First Nations community (Cree) at Calling Lake to teach Sunday school. Later, they helped transport some of the children to the Community Complex, where they began to meet on a regular basis, even hosting over one hundred people one Christmas. Vacation Bible School (VBS) was a regular summer activity, and the Athabasca Reformed Church's youth group also volunteered at Calling Lake on a regular basis.

In 2010, a young couple was hired by the Athabasca Reformed congregation to lead the youth group and to minister in Calling Lake. After they moved on, the work at Calling Lake diminished, but it was revived again when the Athabasca congregation made a new commitment to this ministry under Pastor Al Plat. RCA Global Mission helped develop a new ministry model focusing on ministering *with* the Cree people rather than ministering *to* them. In the spring of 2019, the Athabasca congregation was able to hire a Native American seminary student to help in this ministry.

Summary

The work of Christian mission among Native Americans has been difficult over the years. One of the primary reasons is that through most of the history of White expansion into Native American lands, the Christian churches, including the RCA, have worked closely with the U.S. government in following policies that have been injurious to Native peoples. Because of the close association of churches with anti-Native American practices, many Native Americans still refer to the good news of Jesus Christ as the "White man's gospel."

But there is another side. In Native American communities, which have been battered by centuries of abuse by the dominant culture, by alcohol, by poverty, by family breakdown, and by disillusionment and despair, the Reformed churches continue to bring a message of faith, hope, and love.

In response to today's challenges, leaders of the RCA Native churches have identified two critical areas of training needed by their congregations. The first is to train congregations to go deeper in discipleship, and the second is to empower the next generation of leaders. The decision was made to embark on five learning events spread over two years, in collaboration with the RCA initiative of

Transformed and Transforming, to train the church leaders in how to grow disciples of Jesus and to recruit and empower the next generation of leaders in their communities. This concluded in April of 2020, and the hope is that Native congregations will be better equipped to serve their communities as self-reliant and self-sustaining congregations for the years ahead.

For further reading

Heideman, Eugene. *A People in Mission: Their Expanding Dream*. New York: Reformed Church Press, 1984.

Koopman, LeRoy G. *Taking the Jesus Road: the Ministry of the Reformed Church in America Among Native Americans*. Grand Rapids, MI: Eerdmans, 2005.

CHAPTER 7

Jackson County, Kentucky—1909

Jacob Moss

Jackson County, Kentucky, is part of the region in the United States known as Appalachia. The county was first settled by people of Scottish and Irish descent seeking religious and political liberties and seeking better economic opportunities. As they ventured into Kentucky, they found travel to be difficult because of the steep ridge tops and valleys. As they settled on the hills and in the valleys, the new residents found themselves isolated and this suited them. They cleared enough land to provide for their families and they became self-sufficient. As civilization expanded westward with new roads and railroads, this part of Appalachia was passed by. The new residents lived in a world of their own, preserving many of the customs, speech patterns, and mannerisms of their Elizabethan ancestors, almost forgotten by the rest of the rapidly developing country.

RCA mission work begins in Jackson County, Kentucky

In the late 1800s, the United States was going through a period that Mark Twain called "the Gilded Age." This was a period of rapid industrialization which generated rapid economic growth and improved the quality of life for many Americans. Reports started to surface that the isolated regions of Appalachia were being left far behind in areas of education and living standards from the rest of the country. The Reformed Church in America (RCA) Women's Board of Domestic Missions became interested in helping in Appalachia. They approached William Frost, president of Berea College in Kentucky, to solicit his advice in finding a suitable site to do mission work. He suggested nearby Jackson County. In 1900, New York-based missionaries Cora A. Smith, a teacher and nurse, and Nora Gaut chose McKee as the site of the first RCA mission in Kentucky. Miss Gaut soon had to leave because of illness. But Miss Smith persevered. Outsiders were viewed with suspicion, but over time Smith's nursing skills helped her to gain acceptance. With the help of the Rev. Issac Messler, a church and school were established at McKee, along with several Sunday schools elsewhere in the county.

1n 1906, a second mission station opened in Gray Hawk, a community about six miles east of McKee. Soon, a church was built there, with the Rev. Benjamin DeYoung as pastor. Later, a hospital and a school became part of the mission station. (The hospital closed in 1927 and the school a few years later.)

It was about this time that Kentucky passed a law requiring every county to establish a public school in its county seat. McKee was the county seat for Jackson County, and Messler knew that McKee was not big enough to have two schools. He wrote to the Mission Board and requested permission to sell the McKee school to the county and to use that money to help locate an industrial school nearby. The Mission Board gave its approval. At the same time, William A. Worthington, a widower from Florida, had graduated from New Brunswick Theological Seminary and was pursuing his dream of being a missionary in India. While he was awaiting funds to be secured for that work, the Board asked him to go Kentucky to help Messler secure a site for the new school. Since Messler was an acquaintance of Worthington, he consented and traveled to Kentucky.

Messler and Worthington traveled south of McKee to look over some farmland near Annville. They went to the high point of the property and drew up plans for an industrial school. With the help of additional funds provided by Miss Mary Bussing, the 75-acre farm was purchased. Messler convinced Worthington to stay in Kentucky to start and run the school. Contributing to the decision was the budding romance and later marriage of Worthington and Henrietta Zwemer

Lincoln Hall at Annville Institute,
1909-1921

Tekolste, who was a secretary at the McKee Academy. The couple moved to Annville the day after Christmas in 1909.

Deciding that basic educational skills were more urgently needed than industrial training, the Worthingtons opened the Annville Institute for grades one through eight early in 1910. Annville Institute never became an industrial or technical school, but, under the leadership of the Worthingtons and others, a program was established which aimed at teaching practical as well as academic skills. Worthington described the efforts as providing "complete living for the mountain people." Worthington worked hard to overcome the outsider image. He eventually convinced area residents that the school was not just promoting a "northern religion" but was indeed ecumenical in its mission. By 1924, all twelve grades were being offered, and state accreditation was achieved. Extracurricular offerings included clubs, sports, religious activities, choir, orchestra, a school newspaper, and a literary society. The institute became the cultural hub for the community.

The school's first twenty years saw its most concentrated expansion. The establishment of the Bond Foley Lumber Company and its extension of the railroad from East Bernstadt to Bond, a mile away from Annville, resulted in a sudden population growth that dramatically increased Annville's enrollment between 1914 and 1920. After that time, enrollment leveled off to an average of about 300 students per year until 1931.

By the 1912–13 school year, the entire tract of land except for the campus and a small woodland was being farmed. Male students were involved in farm work and learning programs that emphasized efficient land use, including projects directed at demonstrating the value of advanced methods to local farmers. By 1913, there was also a dairy herd, a pair of registered hogs, a blacksmith shop and small icehouse. By 1930, the school was generating its own electricity, and in addition to the grounds, housing, and classrooms, the physical plant included an infirmary, administrative offices, dining hall, church, workshop, and gymnasium. By 1935, the boys were being trained in agriculture, plumbing, auto mechanics, mechanical drawing, sheet-metal work, and electrical plant operation; the girls received training in weaving, laundry operation, cooking, sewing, canning, and home nursing.

Although religious education and evangelism were always stressed at the school, it was during the Worthington years that evangelism was articulated as being a central part of the education progress: "If we train a student at Annville through regular high school courses only to become a teacher in the state school, our work is in no sense evangelical. However, if we inspire such a student with the desire to become a teacher in the state school in order that he or she may in turn satisfy the desire of pupils for spiritual development, our work is evangelical and such a teacher is just as definitely an evangelist as are we who are in the employment of the mission board."[1]

Meeting the challenges through the years

The 1930s and 1940s were more difficult times for the school. The Great Depression made it necessary to cut the maintenance budget by more than half in 1933. For the duration of the depression years and on into the 1940s, it was not possible to admit as many students or to hire as many staff people as during the earlier, more prosperous years. A notable development of the mid-1930s was the move toward fewer classes, longer class periods, and more hours spent in the work program, with a continued emphasis on extracurricular activities like art, music, and sports. By 1942, the school had stopped offering grades one through seven, but it resumed these grades in 1959.

By the late 1950s, the school had seen several changes. It had weathered the Great Depression but had lost perhaps the most pivotal figures in its history. William Worthington and his wife, Henrietta, had died, and several staff people who held key positions had retired. There continued to be budget problems and questions as to what the primary focus of the RCA work in Jackson County should be. By the late 1940s, the labor program was reported to have become less successful as a bona fide training program than it had been previously, and it had become clear that the program needed to be rejuvenated or discontinued.

The labor program was continued, however, as was the institute's focus on quality academics, extracurricular activities, and Christian evangelism. All of this was still seen as the foundation of the educational and work program. Many former students have said that their most

---

[1]   "Educational Evangelism," scrapbook entry no. 336, January 1940.

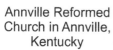

Annville Reformed
Church in Annville,
Kentucky

valuable life lessons came through the work program. Learning how to live one's faith and put that faith into action are common themes that the school's alumni have articulated about their experiences. During the 1950s and 1960s, the dairy herd expanded, and a new Grade A dairy facility was built. Staff members were able to secure donations of equipment and registered dairy heifers. The new facility and up-to-date farming practices helped to develop a good reputation around the farm and the school in the region. The campus hosted several seminars for local farmers. Hundreds of volunteers came from RCA churches to work on campus projects. The volunteers also worked on making needed home repairs in the region. An ambitious outreach program resulted in a total of ten preaching stations throughout the county. Under the leadership of the Rev. Ray Hays, a Jackson County resident who was ordained at the Marble Collegiate Church in New York City, some of the outlying stations grew to be some of the largest congregations in the county. But while the perception in Annville was that the institute was doing great things, there were some undercurrents surfacing that needed to be addressed.

By the 1970s, the public school and transportation systems in the county were improved to the extent that Annville was no longer the singular educational opportunity that it had been for many students during the previous decades. Enrollment began to decrease, and it was becoming increasingly expensive to maintain the physical plant for the relatively small number of students and other program participants. In 1978, the RCA General Program Council (GPC) voted for only what amounted to a basic maintenance budget, making it financially impossible to open school that fall. The closing of the institute caught the community, staff, and students by surprise. It was decided by GPC and classis for reasons of financial efficiency to reduce the number of congregations, combining the ten existing congregations into three located in the three larger communities in the county, Annville, Gray Hawk, and McKee. These decisions, seen as coming from the North, did not go over very well with the citizens of Jackson County. Out of the 100 families that were part of the seven closed congregations, only three families "accepted" a transfer to the remaining three churches. The combination of the closing of the institute and the seven preaching stations caused many Jackson Countians to think that the RCA was abandoning them.

Although the school never reopened, an effort was made to utilize the campus as a place where ministry and outreach could be done. Under the guidance of RCA Global Mission, a nonprofit corporation called Jackson County Ministries (JCM) was organized. JCM was controlled by a board of directors made up mainly of members of the three local RCA congregations remaining in Jackson County. RCA Global Mission continued to provide a major part of the operating funds through contributions coming from RCA churches across the denomination. JCM staff made the decisions to sell off the dairy herd and some excess equipment.

An ambitious outreach program was established during the 1980s. Worthington's motto, "Complete living for the mountain people," was maintained in the campus activities. Programs encouraged students to stay in school with after-school activities. Extremely popular was a mini-bike program that taught mechanical skills and allowed participants to ride motorized bikes through the rolling hills. The program also included counseling and spiritual guidance. In addition, a county wide vacation Bible school (VBS) attracted over 400 students to campus. The students were bussed in every day from all parts of the county to attend the VBS. Such an endeavor would not have been possible except for the many volunteers from Bethany Reformed Church of Des Moines, Iowa. One of the dormitories was converted into an emergency shelter for youth. A small in-ground swimming pool was constructed. This is still the only pool in the county that is available for public swimming. Programs to meet the community's spiritual, physical, and social needs were started. These included a medical clinic, senior citizens' recreational activities, adult education classes, counseling programs, preschool and after-school childcare, a community center at Sand Gap,

and a used clothing store. The programs were effective and filled a need in the area.

In the late 1990s, the old nemesis of insufficient program funding reappeared. Several of the new programs were financed through grants with a time limit on funds. Some of the programs had to be curtailed, and more campus assets were sold to pay off organization obligations. The closing of programs and the sale of more assets caused the feeling of the RCA's having abandoned the area to resurface.

The JCM staff continued the tradition of the institute staff by working with other community leaders and organizations to help promote complete living for area residents. Staff members were instrumental over the years to help establish the Jackson County Health Department (1939), Pond Creek Volunteer Fire Department (1970s), Jackson County Kitchen (2010s) and Little League girls' softball (2010s).

During the 2010s, the campus started to reemerge as a source of community pride. The campground by the pond has been remodeled from just a summer camp into a retreat center that can be used all year. The gym had an addition completed and air conditioning added. The roads and parking lots were resurfaced, and Lincoln Hall, the grand old classroom building on campus, is being renovated into a cultural and event center. These projects were financed by either grants or through special fundraising efforts by the JCM staff.

The situation in Jackson County, Kentucky, today

During the late 2010s, there was a concerted effort to revitalize the image of the RCA's work in Kentucky. There was much discussion

A program called "Get Hooked on Fishing instead of Drugs" teaches youth skills of fishing.

on how the work of the three churches and JCM could be viewed by the community as a combined effort. After much prayer, it was decided to combine the units under the umbrella of a collegiate organization. The name of Grace Covenant Ministries was chosen. So now there is one RCA congregation in Kentucky with three worship centers, each of which have kept the "Reformed" name. Jackson County Ministries, while still maintaining a separate corporate status, accepted the suggestion of changing its name to Grace Covenant Ministries (GCM). This was done to promote a unity of effort within the RCA work in Kentucky. But it also promoted the desire of the organization to reach beyond Jackson County into adjoining areas.

Today, in 2019, the programs of GCM that are mostly funded by RCA churches include summer day camps (sports, arts, and VBS), veteran outreach, thrift stores, youth recreational leagues, the retreat center, and home repair programs. The campus is also home to three other faith-based organizations: the Annville Christian Academy (K-12); Barnabas Home, a residential home for at risk boys; and Lincoln Oaks, a residential treatment center for women trying to overcome addictions. Together, these campus organizations are trying to make a difference, one opportunity at a time, by sharing the love of Christ to those we have been called to serve. Worthington's dream of complete living for the mountain peoples continues.

For further reading

Heideman, Eugene. *A People in Mission: Their Expanding Dream*. New York: Reformed Church Press, 1984.

CHAPTER 8

Southern Normal School, Brewton, Alabama — 1918

Sally Tapley

The founding of Southern Normal School

In the piney woods of southern Alabama once existed an extraordinary school for Black children founded by an extraordinary man, James Dooley. Mr. Dooley, who was born into slavery, was influenced by his mother to be educated. He eventually graduated from Knoxville College as a teacher. He immediately began to look for property to build his school, rooted in the Christian faith, whose mission would be to "educate the heart, head, and hands" of Black students. In 1911, Mr. Dooley found property in Brewton, Alabama, once called the richest little town in the South, that had been a reformatory school for boys. The owners essentially gave the land to him. The property became the Southern Normal School and Industrial Institute, commonly known as Southern Normal School.[1]

---

[1] Aine O'Connor, "Heart, Head, and Hand: James Dooley and Southern Normal School," *Joint Archives of Holland Quarterly* 29, no. 1 (2019): 1-5.

The history of Southern education before integration

To understand the significance of Mr. Dooley's determination to educate Black children, the history of education in the South is important. After the Civil War, the assumption was that everyone was equal in all aspects of civil life. In 1896, the Supreme Court upheld the constitutionality of racial segregation for public facilities as long as they were equal in quality. This became known as the "separate but equal" policy—also known as "separate and *un*equal," especially in education. The counties and cities of the South operated separate schools for Black children through the ninth grade, but there were schools for White students through high school. The amount of money allotted to a Black school was significantly lower. Because much of the South was rural, there was no transportation for Black students, which discouraged many from attending any school.

In order to mitigate the effects of this problem, denominations like the Reformed Church in America and the Methodist Church, along with individuals like James Dooley and Julius Rosenwald, built and supported schools for Black students until integration in the middle of the twentieth century. Although the Supreme Court declared segregation unconstitutional in 1954, actual integration took many years to become a reality due to the resistance of governors and congressmen in states like Alabama. To resist integration, White families organized private "academies," some of which are not integrated to this day. It was 1970 before integration changed the schools in the Brewton area.

During the segregation years, Southern Normal School educated students from Escambia County and the city of Brewton. Because the county and city only operated schools for Black students through ninth grade, they paid a small tuition to Southern Normal School for each Black high school student. In 1960, the county paid $45 a year (the equivalent of $390 today) for a county student to attend Southern Normal School. It was no wonder that Mr. Dooley was constantly struggling for funds to support his school.

The Reformed Church in America and Southern Normal School

Funding was and always would be a struggle throughout the many years of the school's existence. In 1918, Mr. Dooley traveled to the Midwest with the school choir to raise funds. In a small northwest Iowa town, Sioux Center, they came to the attention of the pastor of

The auto shop became an integral part of the industrial training program

First Reformed Church. In the beginning, the church's support came in the form of agricultural equipment and livestock sent to the school by train. Soon, the needs of Mr. Dooley's school were presented to the Board of Domestic Missions of the Reformed Church in America (RCA) by the Classis of Chicago. In 1919, the RCA took on the responsibility of providing funds for the school as a mission of the denomination. Mr. Dooley was named superintendent, and the school was upgraded to meet accreditation standards. It became the first school of its kind in Alabama.

From the beginning, Southern Normal School was both a day and boarding school. Since many students were from rural areas of southern Alabama, it was necessary to offer room and board. Because a train track ran through the property, the train stopped there to drop some students off at school. The school focused on educating the whole life of a student, assuming that some of the students would be farmers and others would go on for more education. Training in the trades became an important part of the curriculum. The school had a working farm that students worked on in order to help pay their tuition. Mary Marshall Tucker relates that students took turns by grade, working for

Southern Normal Institute school bus was used to
transport day students to school

a day, to harvest crops such as corn and blueberries.[2] Almost all of the
food for the students and staff was raised on the farm. If a teacher was
not from Brewton, he or she lived in the dormitory with the students.

Eventually, a primary school was added, named Piney Grove.
Children from the county and city attended. Brenda Stallworth Devroux
attended Southern Normal School from six years of age to high school
graduation. She remembers that there were four classrooms with two
grades in each. The school was heated by a wood burning stove. Several
members of her family were Southern Normal School graduates,
including her father, Eugene Stallworth, in 1932, Brenda in 1962, and
her sister a few years later. She remembers how exciting it was as an
elementary school child to receive Christmas presents sent by Reformed
Church members.[3]

The RCA influence and involvement in the life of Southern
Normal School was deep and extensive throughout its history. The
spiritual aspect of Southern Normal School was unique to Mr. Dooley's
school compared to others founded during this time. Because the RCA

[2]   Mary Marshall Tucker, personal interview by author. Tucker is a graduate of
Southern Normal School (SNS) and Central College in Pella, Iowa. She also taught
at SNS and served as a member of the Board of Trustees.
[3]   Brenda Stallworth Devroux, personal interview by author.

committed to support the school, the reality of segregation became well known to the Midwest churches that provided much of the school's support. Individual churches and members paid scholarships for students. Many buildings on campus were named after Reformed churches and individuals: Bergen Memorial Chapel for Old Bergen Reformed Church in Jersey City, Van Vorst Hall, and Meengs Hall, to name a few.

Reformed Church members also worked and volunteered at the school. Bergen Chapel was organized as a Reformed congregation. Its pastors were also the school chaplains and taught Bible classes. Brenda Stallworth Devroux's family were members of Bergen Chapel. She and her husband, Paul, were married by the Rev. Chet Meengs in Bergen Chapel. Reformed Church members were recruited to teach at the school. The school therefore had an interracial faculty. In order to raise support and thank churches for their support, the Southern Normal School Choir, along with some of its teachers, traveled and visited Reformed churches.

One of the best influences in the relationship between White people and the Black students were the Reformed Church members who volunteered at the school. They came south, especially in the winter months, in their travel trailers, or they lived in the dorm with the students. They performed maintenance, painted, tutored, and generally acted as grandparents to the students living in the dorms. For the students and volunteers alike, this was the first interaction with the other race. This gave them all an opportunity to get to know each other, benefitting the students when they entered the larger world of an integrated society away from the South.

Twice a year, RCA pastors and often their families came to the school to conduct Religious Emphasis Week and the Spring Youth Conference. Mary Tucker especially remembers the closing service as students walked through the campus with candles. A Reformed Church program for teens, Caravan, visited the school, and Southern Normal students annually took part in a "Caravan" to the Annville Institute in Kentucky.

The secretary of the Board of Domestic Missions of the Reformed Church had oversight of several Reformed Church missions, including Jackson County Ministries, also known as Anneville Institute; Native American ministries; and Southern Normal School. The secretary hired the staff after Mr. Dooley's passing in 1930. One notable secretary was Dr. Beth Marcus. She was beloved by the students and staff because she visited the campus several weeks a year. She encouraged and supported the staff and students by finding opportunities for further education for staff and graduates. One effort of hers that stands out was her recognition that the school needed a gymnasium. Enough funds were raised from the churches to build the finest one in the area.[4]

The Reformed Church colleges and Southern Normal School

A special program of Southern Normal School with the Reformed Church was the opportunity for Southern Normal graduates to attend one of the three Reformed Church colleges: Northwestern College and Central College in Iowa and Hope College in Holland, Michigan. For most of the years of Southern Normal's existence, its students were offered reduced tuition or tuition-free enrollment in these colleges. Imagine what it must have been like for Mary Marshall Tucker and her two sisters to leave rural Alabama by train in the late 1940s, to cross the Mason-Dixon line, to sit where they wanted, to see snow for the first time, to be usually treated the same as everyone, and to enroll in Central College in Pella, Iowa. She explains that this opportunity affected her and her family for their entire lives. After graduating from Central College, she returned to Southern Normal School to teach history, marry, and raise four children in Monroeville, Alabama. A *Church Herald* article in 1951 says that there were seventeen teachers on the staff of Southern Normal School, ten of whom were Southern Normal graduates and three of whom were Central College graduates.[5] Tucker believes her children benefitted greatly by the visits of her college friends and their families. Living in the south, three of her four children attended segregated schools. Some Southern Normal School students never interacted with White folks other than Reformed Church volunteers before graduating and moving away from the South. The last Southern Normal student to attend Hope College graduated in the early 1990s. One student who had a great impact on the school and the Reformed Church was the Rev. Sam Williams. After graduating from Southern Normal School, he attended Northwestern College and graduated from Central College and Western Theological Seminary. He returned to Southern Normal as chaplain and teacher, as did his wife, Pauline, who was the first African American female graduate of

4   James Baar, "A Letter from 'Gym' Baar," *The Church Herald*, November 5, 1965, 12–13.

5   Mary Louise Marshall, "The Educational Program at Southern Normal School," *The Church Herald*, November 23, 1951, 19.

Hope College. They served several Reformed churches before retiring to Brewton. James Carter Dooley, the son of the founder, was the first African American to graduate from Hope College in 1932. Many Southern Normal graduates became teachers.

The impact of integration

While students benefitted greatly from a Christ-centered education at Southern Normal School, the United States was convulsing in the change from segregation to integration. This reality was a struggle for the students as well.

Known by all who loved her as "Miss Hollinger," Ida Mae Hollinger was a teacher at Southern Normal throughout the 1950s. Aine O'Connor quotes an article from the *Church Herald* in which Ida Mae wrote, "God has become to me big enough to embrace all mankind—all races, all nations. He is not that large to many of the [Black] youth with whom we work."[6] Ida Mae's message might have been hard to accept by most of the *Church Herald* readers at the time, but it was fundamentally necessary for everyone to understand just how much Southern Normal students went through for an education.

O'Connor continues with Ida Mae's thoughts: "The pupils read about Christianity and American democracy but they live with the practice of white supremacy."[7] All students had to recognize their inherent value and worth within a Christian context to move forward in learning. One of the school's greatest triumphs would be to convince scores of young children of color that God loved them deeply as themselves." In her *Church Herald* article, Ida Mae wrote, "In the midst of this hypocritical society with its oppression and associates: poverty, ignorance, superstition, filth, immorality and hate, Southern Normal stands as a light and haven of freedom and justice, of love and mercy."[8] When asked if Southern Normal still mattered as integration became law, most Southern Normal School administrators answered that only at Southern Normal could Black students get a Christ-centered education, be guided and motivated by a Christian interracial faculty, and study and work in an atmosphere of love. The school was a safe place, and students wanted to be there because the school recognized their value.

---

[6]   Aine O'Connor, "Heart, Head, and Hand," 4.
[7]   Ida Mae Hollinger, "Is God Prejudiced Too?" *The Church Herald*, March 14, 1958, 22.
[8]   Hollinger, "Is God Prejudiced Too?" 22.

Rottschafer Preschool children are ready for activities
in the basement of Bergen Chapel.

Rottschafer Day Care Center

In 1967, in the basement of Bergen Chapel, Mary Ann McMillan
of Brewton opened a preschool for Black children. Volunteers,
including Marjorie Rottschafer of Grand Rapids, Michigan, spent
the winter living in the girls' dorm to assist in the preschool. In 1992,
the preschool moved into the former director's home on campus.
Reformed Church volunteers rebuilt the home to be a state-licensed,
certified preschool. Today, the Rottschafer Day Care Center meets in
a new, licensed building close to the former campus. Florence Rowser
continues to be the director, and she has a passion for the youngest
and neediest children of the Brewton area, a lasting legacy of Southern
Normal School and the Reformed Church in America.[9]

The impact of integration was profound on Southern Normal
School. In 1968, the RCA decided to establish an independent advisory
board to operate the school. One third of this board comprised Brewton
community members, and another third members of the RCA. The RCA

---

[9]   Lois M. Joice, "Happiness Is The R.C.A. Kindergarten in Brewton," *The Church
Herald*, December 13, 1968, 11; Florence Rowser, personal interview with author.
Rowser taught at SNS and was the director of the Rottschafer Day Care Center.

was still fully committed to financially support the school, but it also believed it was time for the school to establish a wider support base.

The final chapter

Enrollment began to slowly decline after integration had occurred in public schools. As the county and city accepted the responsibility of educating all students, more parents chose to send their children to integrated schools. At its peak, Southern Normal School had 350 students. The board and administration tried to expand the mission of the school to attract students from urban schools that were not providing a quality education. It became apparent that parents did not wish to send their children to a boarding school. The facilities also needed to be upgraded, and the curriculum was not meeting the needs of the digital age.

With great sadness and reluctance, the board of trustees decided to close the school in 1997. The property was sold to Alabama State University in hopes that the university would be able to use the facilities for satellite learning. Unfortunately, the school property remains unused today.

Many Southern Normal School graduates have testified to the impact of the Reformed Church on their lives. Without the Reformed Church in America's support of Southern Normal School, many would not have had the opportunity to graduate from school, attend college and graduate school, or leave the segregated South. As alumnus and attorney Carl Singley told *The New York Times*, "What the school gave to us was structure and discipline and a set of values."[10] Many graduates became educators, including Dr. Manford Byrd, the former Chicago superintendent of schools, and Paul Adams of the renowned Providence St. Mel School in Chicago. Dr. Manford Byrd, Jr. wrote in a *Church Herald* article in 1967, "Where I would be today without the experience of attending Southern Normal School is hard to contemplate. Southern Normal was the educational oasis for me, and other Negro boys and girls like me, in the educational desert of North Escambia County, Alabama."[11]

Brenda Devroux says it well: "The wingspan of the Reformed Church was very wide. The church gave us self respect and one up on

[10] Peter Applebome, "Boarding Schools for Blacks Are Having a Resurgence in Popularity," *The New York Times*, September 21, 1994, section B, 12.
[11] Manford Byrd Jr., "A Time To Remember," *The Church Herald*, December 22, 1967, 17.

life." Thanks to the faithful determination of a son of slavery, hundreds of young people realized his dream to educate their hearts, heads and hands.

For further reading

Applebome, Peter. "Boarding Schools for Blacks Are Having a Resurgence in Popularity" *The New York Times*, September 21, 1994, section B, 12.

Baar, James. "A Letter from 'Gym' Baar." *The Church Herald*. November 5, 1965.

Byrd, Manford Jr. "A Time To Remember." *The Church Herald*. December 22, 1967.

Heideman, Eugene. *A People in Mission: Their Expanding Dream,* New York: Reformed Church Press, 1984.

Hollinger, Ida. "Is God Prejudiced Too?" *The Church Herald*. March 14, 1958.

Joice, Lois M. "Happiness Is The R.C.A. Kindergarten in Brewton." *The Church Herald*. December 13, 1968.

Marshall, Mary Louise. "The Educational Program at Southern Normal School," *The Church Herald*, November 23, 1951.

O'Connor, Aine. "Heart, Head, and Hand: James Dooley and Southern Normal School." *Joint Archives of Holland Quarterly* 29, no. 1 (2019): 1-5.

CHAPTER 9

Chiapas—1925

J. Samuel Hofman and Jean Van Engen

The State of Chiapas in southern Mexico is about half the size of Iowa. It is a remote, green jewel snuggled up against Guatemala, and is similar to it both geographically and culturally. In 1824, following the war of independence in which both Mexico and Guatemala broke free from Spain, Chiapas chose to become part of Mexico.

Chiapas is a rugged mountainous area, kept lush and green by heavy rainfall coming from three directions: from the Pacific, from the Caribbean, and from the north. The gospel also came to Chiapas from three directions: from Mexico City, from Guatemala, and from Tabasco, the state to the northeast of Chiapas. Chiapas was a spiritually parched land. The Catholic Church had a monopoly dating back to the Spanish conquest in the 1520s. The Catholicism that arrived was medieval Catholicism, unchallenged and unrefined by the Reformation and the Renaissance. In the centuries that followed, the remoteness and ruggedness of Chiapas, the scarcity of priests, and the illiteracy of the people produced a mix of Catholicism and traditional animist beliefs.

From 1902 to 1904, visits to Chiapas by English missionaries from Mexico City succeeded in planting seeds in Tuxtla Gutierrez, the

Map of Chiapas showing the location of churches of the
National Presbyterian Church of Mexico in 1965

capital city in central Chiapas. But the chaos of the Mexican Revolution
that erupted in 1910 made further visits impossible.

At the same time, the gospel was brought from Guatemala to
southern Chiapas by Mayan workers, who had been converted through
Presbyterian mission work in Guatemala. They placed Bibles in the
hands of the town officials in the village of Mazapa. The president and
secretary of the village were converted, and this humble highland village
became a beacon of light for that area. Guatemalan coffee pickers also
brought the gospel to coffee ranches near the town of Tapachula, and
a congregation formed in this commercial center at the end of the
railroad.

Joseph Coffin, originally from Kentucky, married a Mexican
woman and settled in Tabasco. They had a son, José, whom they

dedicated to the Lord's service. José went to Presbyterian Theological Seminary in Mexico City, where he met and married an educated and dedicated young woman, Luz Otero. After his graduation, they returned in 1905 to serve in remote Tabasco.

In 1920, José Coffin accompanied one of the Tabascan ministers, the Rev. Eligio Granados, on a trip into Chiapas. Their preaching in the village of Tumbalá was rewarded by a large number of converts, including both Spanish-speaking ranchers and Ch'ol-speaking laborers.

The believers in Tapachula, the southern tip of Chiapas, had multiplied quickly. Hearing that there were other Presbyterians in Mexico City, they sent word to them asking for pastoral help. Responding to the request, the Presbyterian leaders in Tabasco decided to send José Coffin and his wife to Tapachula, where they built a chapel and parsonage and started medical work, six primary schools, and a community Red Cross office. José Coffin organized three additional congregations and was visiting families and groups of believers in eighty-one locations scattered throughout the interior of Chiapas.

How and with whom the RCA first got involved

The heavy workload prompted Coffin to request missionary help from the Presbyterian Mission Board, but they responded that they were already overextended. However, the Presbyterian Mission Board in turn invited the Reformed Church in America to provide a missionary for Chiapas. The Board of Foreign Missions of the RCA responded that they also were already overextended.

The Reformed Church Women's Board of Domestic Missions heard of the opportunity, and they accepted the challenge. They justified their beginning a ministry in this foreign land by saying that, from their perspective, work among the Mayan peoples of Chiapas would be an extension of their mission work among the Native Americans in the United States.

The Men's Board of Domestic Missions agreed to join them in investigating this opportunity. An investigative committee of four made the long trip from New York to Tapachula in 1925. The trip included a long cruise from New York to Veracruz and a slow train trip to the southern tip of Chiapas. The committee was made up of Mrs. Edith A. Allen and Mrs. Ada Quimby Knox of the Women's Board and the Rev. G. Watermulder and the Rev. Henry Sluyter of the Board of Domestic Missions.

José Coffin, an ardent Presbyterian, was not pleased when he heard that instead of missionaries from the Presbyterian Church, he was being offered aid from the RCA, which he suspected as being much too liberal. But his concern was eased when he found that one of the women had the name of Mrs. Ada Knox, the same last name as the revered Presbyterian reformer John Knox. The Coffins were so impressed by her that they named the playground of their school Ada Park.

Mrs. Allen was also very impressed. Upon return to the U.S., she wrote a report of their trip and their visit with the Coffins, including this sentence which gives a blueprint for the future work in Chiapas:

> "Shall the Reformed Church in America come to the help of this noble servant of the Master and send preachers, medical workers and such native helpers as may be, to some well chosen and equipped Reformed Church Mission center in Chiapas, to be associated with the Presbyterian forces there in bringing Chiapas into that fellowship of Christ through which in His own time it will itself be able to achieve entirely, not only its own Christian ministry, but also send gospel messengers to [indigenous peoples] of other more remote sections of South America where millions wait the gospel of a Saviour's love and healing?"

She answers her question enthusiastically:

> The Domestic Boards have said 'Yes' to this call from Over the Border, and some in our churches by their gifts have also said 'Yes.' A noble young son of the Church and recent graduate of Princeton, with his prospective bride, have answered 'Here I am, send me' - and they are going - and we are going - all of us - through prayer and love and gifts, for the Reformed Church in America does not put its hand to the plow and hesitate. It does not fail. Yes, in Christ's name and in His power we are coming to help you, [brothers and sisters in] Chiapas! We are coming, honored brother José Coffin, and all other lovers of the Master there whose names we know not yet. Blessed, heavenly Father, lead thou us on that Thy will may have its way with us for Chiapas and all the great work to which Domestic Missions is called.[1]

Thus began the collaboration of the Reformed Church in America with the National Presbyterian Church of Mexico.

---

[1]   *The Christian Intelligencer and Mission Field*, June 3, 1925, 341.

The first RCA missionaries to Chiapas

The "recent graduate of Princeton" was John R. Kempers. Growing up in Sioux Center, Iowa, he served one summer at the Comanche Indian Mission of Lawton, Oklahoma, under the Rev. Richard Harper, who recommended him to the Domestic Board for this new venture in Chiapas. John's "prospective bride" was Mabel Van Dyke of Holland, Michigan, who was a graduate of Hope College. Following John's graduation, they were married in August of 1925.

On December 4, the Kempers took the same cruise to Veracruz, arriving on December 12. Two weeks later the door closed behind them. The Mexican government began enforcing some of the anti-church laws of the liberal constitution, prohibiting the entrance of foreign ministers and priests into Mexico. Foreign priests and ministers living in Mexico could no longer serve the sacraments. Hundreds of priests and nuns were expelled from the country, beginning a long and sometimes violent chapter of conflict between the state and the church in Mexico.

After some orientation and language study in Jalapa and Mexico City, the Kempers took the long train ride to Tapachula, arriving on May 1, 1926. Their assignment was to reach the peoples of Chiapas. There were six tribes scattered in the state. José Coffin proposed that he and John Kempers, known as Kemp, make an exploratory trip through the state, beginning at the northern border and traveling south through the state to Tapachula. Coffin intimated that it would be a two-week trip.

Coffin was testing the Kemperses' commitment and endurance. Leaving their wives in torrid Tapachula, they took the train north and east to Tabasco, where Coffin spent two weeks visiting family and the congregations there. Kemp wrote to Mabel, warning her that the trip was going to take longer than two weeks, and expressing his regret that he would not be with her to celebrate their first wedding anniversary.

They purchased horses and mules and supplies and began the trail into Chiapas. It was the middle of rainy season, the worst time of the year to travel. The trails were horrendous, the mosquitoes ferocious. They visited some of the groups of believers on the way in Tumbalá, Yajalón, and Chilón, and they replaced their worn-out horses five times. Kemp nearly died from food poisoning halfway home in the town of Ocosingo. God provided help from an American doctor who happened to be there. A few days later, in Comitán, Coffin became seriously ill with dysentery. Two months after they had left home, the bedraggled pair rode slowly into Tapachula.

Both Kemp and Mabel passed the first test. Instead of calling the assignment impossible, they took as their motto: *Chiapas para Cristo* (Chiapas for Christ). They now knew how challenging it would be. As Kemp wrote: "If it takes two months to cross the state, how long will it take to cover it?"

Kemp decided that their first priority should be to strengthen the Spanish-speaking believers, in hopes that these Mexican believers would later reach out to the Mayan tribes around them. On the trip he had seen Ch'ol converts in the congregations in Tumbalá and Yajalón. He hoped this would happen in other places as well. So Kemp joined Coffin, with their saddle horses and mules, in the visitation of the scattered Mexican believers as their partners in mission. Years later, in retirement, Kemp wrote: "I wish all the Chiapas missionaries would get on their horses and visit the churches in their areas. I know from experience how important that is. There was a time when I knew every believer in Chiapas and everyone knew me. I often traveled two days up and two days back just to visit one family."[2]

The Kempers moved to the capital city of Tuxtla Gutierrez in central Chiapas in 1931. There they began working with groups of believers who had first been evangelized nearly thirty years before by the missionaries from Mexico City. The Tuxtla congregation developed quickly to the point where they called a Mexican minister, the Rev. Ezequiel Lango, from Mexico City to serve them. The work was strengthened by Lango's ministry, and eventually the Presbytery of the Gulf gave him the pastoral responsibility for all of the central area of the state.

In the early 1940s, Mexico's political leaders relaxed their anti-church prohibitions and the door to missionaries opened slightly. Garold and Ruth Van Engen were sent as the second RCA missionary family, entering Mexico in 1943. They went to the town of Yajalón to prepare to serve the Ch'ol converts in that area. The tropical climate quickly undermined Ruth's health, and the doctor urged them to return to the U.S. or at least find a cooler climate. In 1948, they moved to the city of San Cristóbal de Las Casas, located at an elevation of 7,000 feet. There they teamed up with a dynamic, capable Mexican minister, the Rev. Daniel Aguilar Ochoa. Together, they developed a Bible school and established a printing press for religious publications.

In the mid-1940s, Mexico was the first challenge for Wycliffe Bible Translators. Their missionaries entered the six tribes of Chiapas, living

[2]   John Kempers to Sam Hofman, September 23, 1971.

In 1959 six RCA couples were serving in Chiapas: (*l. to r.*)
Al and Nita DeVoogd, John and Mabel Kempers, Sam and
Helen Hofman, Henry and Char Stegenga, Garold and
Ruth Van Engen, and Paul and Dorothy Meyerink

in remote villages in order to learn their languages. To provide them
with transportation, supplies, and communication, a new organization
of Christian pilots and mechanics called Mission Aviation Fellowship
(MAF) arrived in Chiapas. They established a base in central Chiapas
at Ixtapa with two airplanes. For thirty-eight years, MAF provided
transportation and communication for the missionaries of Chiapas
without suffering a serious injury or fatal accident.

The Ch'ol and Tzeltal tribes responded enthusiastically to
the ministry of the Wycliffe missionaries, who completed their New
Testament translations in the 1950s. Four new RCA missionary couples
arrived to establish Bible schools for the training of the church leaders,
the production of literature and visual aids, and the continuation of
village medical work in those tribal areas. By 1959, a group of six couples
formed the Chiapas Mission. For the Kempers it meant additional work
in communication, orientation, and the complicated struggle to get
immigration papers for the new couples. Their home in the capital city
became the refuge for renewal and shopping for the four couples living
in the remote tribal areas.

Whereas the Ch'ol and Tzeltal believers multiplied very rapidly,
the progress in the Tzotzil and Tojolabal tribes was much slower.
This was due to severe persecution. Tribal and village authorities
were determined not to permit any change from their animistic

Catholicism. The initial persecution in the Ch'ol and Tzeltal tribes subsided quite quickly, but in the Tzotzil and Tojolabal tribes, the persecution was persistent and violent. Wycliffe missionaries and their converts were chased out of the villages. The Tzotzil Christian refugees began accumulating in San Cristobal and the Tojolabal refugees in Las Margaritas. The translations of the New Testaments continued, and eventually the Wycliffe missionaries and their Mayan translation partners produced New Testaments in Tojolabal and in five dialects of the Tzotzil language.

In the heat of the persecution, it was the Mexican Presbyterian Church leaders and believers who came to the aid of the persecuted indigenous believers. As the Wycliffe missionaries completed their translations and moved on, the Tzotzil and Tojolabal believers asked the Presbyterian leaders to receive and organize them. This helped in their relationship to regional and state government officials, as the Presbyterian Church was recognized and respected. This also provided the opportunity for additional RCA missionaries to serve in the Tzotzil and Tojolabal fields. At the same time, others arrived to continue the training of leaders for the Spanish-speaking churches. During the 1970s, the size of the Chiapas Mission reached ten couples working with the Spanish-speaking churches and with the believers in four of the state's Mayan groups.

The primary types of ministries completed by RCA missionaries

The missionaries majored in leadership development in the Spanish-speaking churches and in churches speaking four Mayan languages they worked with, establishing a seminary, five Bible schools, and a paramedic training center. Translation work included Bibles (Old and revised New Testaments) in five different languages or dialects and a New Testament. Work was done on the preparation and publication of hymnals, concordances, textbooks, pamphlets, Sunday school materials, and news bulletins in five languages. Collaborative work was also done in evangelism, medical support, youth and women's work, music, and aid to persecuted believers and Guatemalan refugees, alongside national pastors and leaders in each language group.

Missionary service in Chiapas was characterized by long-term service. The first six couples each averaged over thirty years in Chiapas. The next eight couples averaged over seventeen years of service. This was in spite of the serious health hazards that sent several couples home sooner than anticipated. This long-term commitment provided

The first Chiapas Presbytery was formed in 1948. Seated in the front row are (*l. to r.*) Garold Van Engen, the 5 newly ordained pastors needed to form a presbytery (called classis in the RCA) and John Kempers.

continuity and productivity for the work. RCA missionary couples invested a total of 350 years of service in Chiapas. That represented a huge amount of financial and prayer support from the RCA, living up to Mrs. Allen's expectations when she wrote, "The Reformed Church in America does not put its hand to the plow and hesitate. It does not fail."[3]

The situation in Chiapas today

Almost one hundred years have now passed since the Kempers arrived in Chiapas. The scattered groups of believers then totaled less than 1,000. Today, the National Presbyterian Church in Chiapas has grown to be larger than the Reformed Church in America, with over 350,000 members, gathering in at least 2,000 church buildings and worshipping in six languages. This brings to reality the Kempers' challenge—*Chiapas para Cristo*, Chiapas for Christ.

---

[3]   Edith H. Allen, "Seen and Felt in Mexico," *The Christian Intelligencer and Mission Field* 96, no. 22 (1925): 341.

Editors' update:

As of 2020, the RCA is involved in many mission partnerships and varied ministries throughout Latin America and the Caribbean. The reader can access information regarding the RCA's work in Latin America at rca.org/mission.

- Brazil
- Colombia
- Dominican Republic
- Guatemala
- Haiti
- Honduras
- Jamaica
- Latin American Doctoral Program in Theology
- Mexico
- Nicaragua
- Peru

Further Reading

Allen, Edith H. "Seen and Felt in Mexico." *The Christian Intelligencer and Mission Field* 96, no. 22 (1925): 341.

"Charm and Challenge of Chiapas." *Annual Publication of the Chiapas Mission, 1955 to 1992,* New York: Reformed Church in America Press.

Deiros, Pablo. *Kemp: The Story of John R. and Mabel Kempers, Founders of the Reformed Church in America Mission in Chiapas, Mexico.* The Historical Series of the Reformed Church in America. Grand Rapids, MI: Eerdmans, 2016.

Heideman, Eugene. *A People in Mission: Their Expanding Dream.* New York: Reformed Church Press, 1984.

Hofman, J. Samuel. *Mission Work in Today's World.* Pasadena, CA: William Carey Library, 1993.

Meyerink, Dorothy D. *Ministry Among the Maya: A Missionary Memoir.* The Historical Series of the Reformed Church in America. Grand Rapids, MI: Eerdmans, 2011.

Reformed Review 58, no. 1 (2004). This entire journal issue is dedicated to articles by Roger De Young, J. Samuel Hofman, Vernon J. Sterk, and Charles E. Van Engen about mission work in Chiapas.).

Sterk, Vernon J. *Surviving Persecution: How to Understand, Prepare and Respond.* Eugene, OR: Wipf and Stock, 2019.

Van Engen, Charles E. *Misión y Comisión: historias de mi tierra.* Lima, Peru: CENIP, 2014. (Only available in Spanish.)

CHAPTER 10

Africa—1946

Derrick Jones

The Reformed Church in America began its ministry in Africa in 1948 with the arrival of three missionaries into Sudan. The Christian presence in Sudan dates back to the third century, when Coptic Christians held significant influence in the kingdom of Merowe in Nubia. Tradition has it that Queen Candace of Merowe was converted by the preaching of her state treasurer, the Ethiopian eunuch who had met Philip on the road from Jerusalem to Gaza (Acts 8:26-40). This witness led to the conversion of many in the region of Nubia. The introduction of Orthodox Melkite tradition by a Nubian bishop in about 1000 A.D. provoked a split between the Church in Nubia and the Coptic Church in Egypt. Although this split occurred, Christianity continued to flourish in Sudan until the fourteenth century, when Islam ascended and ultimately extinguished all Christian presence.[1]

In 1842, the modern era of Christian mission activity began when the Roman Catholic Church sent missionaries to Sudan. The Anglicans and American Presbyterians entered Sudan in 1899. The Anglican

[1]   James A. Cogswell, *No Turning Back: A History of American Presbyterian Involvement in Sub-Saharan Africa 1833–2000.* (Philadelphia: Xlibris Corporation, 2007), 22-23.

missionaries from the Church Missionary Society began sharing the gospel and set up a base in Omdurman, near the capital city of Khartoum, followed by the American Presbyterian Mission. The pioneer American Presbyterian missionary Rev J. Kelly Giffen, from the United Presbyterian Church of North America (UPNA), entered Sudan under the auspices and in collaboration with the Arabic-speaking Evangelical Church of Egypt (ECE). With a commitment and passion to proclaim the gospel, the ECE adopted the Muslim Sudan in the north as its sphere of missionary enterprise. By 1901, in the town of Omdurman, Egyptian members of the Evangelical Church of Egypt working in Sudan formed a small congregation led by an Evangelical Egyptian pastor, the Rev. Gebra Hanna. This became the base of the work in the north, which gradually expanded to Khartoum and Khartoum North with a focus on education, medical work, and women's Bible training.

In 1902, shortly after the establishment of the church in the north, the Rev. and Mrs. Giffen ventured south with Dr. and Mrs. H. T. McLaughlin to work among the Nilotic tribes scattered through the forests and marshy plains in the extremely primitive areas of the Upper Nile Province. They established a mission station in Doleib Hill at the convergence of the White Nile and the Sobat Rivers, near the city of Malakal. They focused on reaching the Shilluk people by doing linguistic work to develop the written language, establishing a literacy program, and providing basic medical care.

In the north, the focus remained on providing Arabic schools for Egyptian Christians and reaching out to the larger non-Christian community. By 1936, the Evangelical Church grew to a few hundred, with six ordained pastors serving nine congregations, plus a number of preaching points not fully organized. In the south, the focus was on reaching the African Nilotic tribes. The missionaries used the rivers as highways of travel to work among the tribal village people along the Sobat and Pibor rivers.[2]

How and with whom the RCA first got involved

In 1938, the American Presbyterian mission launched a major campaign to reach the Anuak people in southeastern Sudan. They received land and opened a station in Akobo near the Ethiopian border. Unfortunately, this work was short-lived, because the Italian invasion of Ethiopia resulted in battles between British forces and the Italians

2   Cogswell, *No Turning Back*, 21–26.

along the Sudan-Ethiopia border. Port Sudan, which was the port of entry for most supplies and missionaries coming to Sudan, was bombed repeatedly and eventually closed. These tensions led to the evacuation of mission personnel from Akobo, leaving the mission station unoccupied. These battles impacted Sudan from 1940 to 1942. The work in Akobo did not resume until 1944, when a serious famine broke out in the south, particularly in the area of the Anuaks. Over the course of the next year, a surprising harvest was realized. At the Christmas gathering, twenty-five Anuaks were baptized into the Christian faith, and the first Anuak church was organized in 1945 with the ordination of three elders. A great door had opened, and there was much excitement and promise for the work among the Anuak and other areas throughout the south.[3]

In 1945, the Reformed Church in America (RCA) began to discuss the possibility of merging with the UPNA. As a part of this process, the United Presbyterians invited the RCA to join them in their long history of mission in the Anglo-Egyptian Sudan in Africa. In 1946, the Foreign Missions of the Presbyterian Church forwarded the invitation and recommendation to the Board of Foreign Missions of the Reformed Church in America to join them in mission by appointing missionaries to work among the Anuaks in southern Sudan.

The Rev. Don McClure, the veteran missionary who opened the initial Presbyterian work to the Anuaks, made a profound impression on RCA churches, colleges, seminaries and the Board of Foreign Missions. The United Presbyterian's invitation to engage in mission in Sudan was enthusiastically endorsed by RCA leaders and was accepted after careful consideration and full consultation with the General Synod. In introducing this new mission field, the RCA Board of Foreign Missions wrote,

> It is this type of comprehensive approach which the Rev. Donald McClure and his colleagues have been employing with the Anuak tribe in the South Sudan and it is this kind of inclusive program which the Reformed Church hopes to carry on among another tribe still to be designated, possibly the Murle.
>
> The Reformed Church traditionally has cooperated with other groups on the mission fields; it has never sought to perpetuate its own organization or institutions but has helped to build a church rooted in the land and suited to the culture of the people.

[3]　Cogswell, *No Turning Back*, 41–42, 87–88.

That is its plan again in this instance. No new machinery is to be created or elaborate building erected. The main emphasis will be on the contribution of personnel, consecrated, trained missionary recruits. They will be named and trained by our church but serve in the Sudan Mission already at work. Evangelists will be needed, teachers, doctors, specialists in Christian education, child welfare, agriculture, and the like, so that an all-round ministry may be offered – and introduction to that abundant life on Christ Jesus.

It was ten years before the United Presbyterians baptized their first convert. Now, there are well established congregations, made up of clean-living, God-fearing, consecrated Christian folk. It is our hope to bring some other tribe in Sudan similar opportunities. The evangelization of the whole tribe- that is our aim, and then another and yet another tribe. ... The church is eager to go forward. Prayers, gifts, lives will be needed if we are indeed to go in and possess the land.[4]

Having a shared mission philosophy and principles with the United Presbyterians coupled with the clear leading of the Spirit, it was a natural fit for the RCA to positively respond to the opportunity to enter this new field in the Sudan. Thus, the RCA agreed to work cooperatively with UPNA towards the evangelization of South Sudan, which was comprised of traditional indigenous tribes who were completely without the gospel.

The first RCA missionaries to Africa

The first RCA missionary to be appointed to this new field in Africa was Ms. Wilma Kats. She was a native of Nebraska and a graduate of Central College. In 1946, at the time of her appointment, she was serving as a primary school teacher in Denver, Colorado. She had a passion for teaching and a deep sense of call to venture beyond that which was familiar and to follow Christ to reach the peoples of Sudan.

The Rev. Robert "Bob" Swart, a native of DeMotte, Indiana, and his wife, Morrel ("Morrie"), a native of Flushing, New York, were the next missionaries to be appointed to serve in Sudan. They were both Hope College graduates. After Bob's graduation from Western Theological Seminary (WTS), Bob and Morrie were married in June of 1944. He

4   Board of Foreign Missions, RCA, 1946, Joint Archives of Holland, Hope College, Holland, MI.

accepted the call to serve as the pastor of the Grace Reformed Church in Fond du Lac, Wisconsin. During their tenure at Hope College and WTS, they heard many missionaries' stories of how God was at work around the world. They had discerned God's call to mission but were not sure when and how it would materialize. The new venture of the RCA in Sudan presented an opportunity and call beyond Morrie's initial imagination and comfort zone. However, after working through her apprehension about Africa, the Swarts fully submitted to God's call on their lives and accepted the opportunity to serve as missionaries to Sudan. In the fall of 1947, they were commissioned by Bob's home church, the American Reformed Church in DeMotte, Indiana.

In January of 1948, with support of many congregations within the RCA, the Swart family and Wilma Kats set sail on the old Italian ship called the *Saturnia* with Don and Lydia McClure to serve as pioneer missionaries to Sudan. It was a three-month journey sailing to Egypt, traveling by train to Khartoum, flying from Khartoum to Malakal, and then driving to Akobo. They arrived on April 5, 1948.

The Rev. Harvey Hoekstra, a native of Minnesota, and Mrs. Lavina Hoekstra, a native of Holland, Michigan, were also appointed to serve as pioneer missionaries to Sudan. Harvey and Lavina met while he was a student at Hope College, and they later married. It was during his senior year at WTS that he heard "a red headed, rash, religious Presbyterian missionary on furlough at morning chapel. He had recently come from South Sudan in Africa. He said he was looking for new missionary recruits to join him at Akobo in the Sudan." After chapel, Harvey had a discussion with Don McClure about how he could use his gifts and passion for languages by possibly becoming a Bible translator on their team. Discerning God's call, upon returning home, he immediately told his wife, "Honey, we are going to Africa."[5] Like their predecessors, they received the full support of RCA congregations and the Women's Board of Foreign Missions and were commissioned for service. On July 2, 1948, the Hoekstras set sail for Sudan and soon joined the team in Akobo.

Upon arrival, RCA missionaries immediately began learning the language and becoming immersed in the culture and customs of the Anuak with the rest of the team. Unlike other Nilotic tribes in that area, which were primarily pastoralist, the Anuak were farmers living along the banks and rivers of South Sudan and western Ethiopia. They

---

[5]   This was the initial title of the book by Harvey T. Hoekstra, which was later republished with the title *From "Knotted Strings" to Talking Bibles*.

shared a common origin with their northern neighbors, the Shilluk, and a similar language to their neighbors to the south, the Acholi. They grew most of their own food and lived in independent, self-sufficient, and isolated villages away from other Anuak peoples. Each village was led by a headman who governed and oversaw the village ceremonies.

After more than a year in the field, the missionaries and Anuaks at the Akobo mission station seemed to be in a spiritual rut, with little outward response to the preaching and teaching of the Word of God. Then, the East Africa Revival, which contributed to the significant growth of the church in East Africa from the 1940s to the 1970s, reached southern Sudan through an inconspicuous, unlikely medium. Revival was sparked when Captain Richard Lyth, the British district commissioner, and his family returned from vacation in Uganda. During a Sunday service, using themes of "brokenness" and "walking in the light," he quietly shared about the spiritual truths and teachings he learned while fellowshipping with the spiritually vibrant church in Uganda. In his brokenness of spirit, having already confessed his sins before God, he confessed them before the entire congregation, which comprised missionaries, his colleagues, his employees, and African students and teachers. The Holy Spirit was powerfully present, impacting all, and many other confessions followed in subsequent meetings.[6] A spirit of confession, repentance, new life, and revival emerged in the church among the Anuaks. With this new sense of fervor and commitment to Christ, the schoolboys began to openly and boldly share their faith in Christ, launching an evangelistic campaign to win all the people in the villages for Christ. Morrie Swart stated,

> The swift positive impact of the power of the Holy Spirit in the lives of the Anuaks was an almost incredible fact. But the story didn't end there. The missionaries themselves, as a group, experienced spiritual cleansing such as we had never known before.
>
> We had met together for our usual Thursday evening prayer meeting, but God made it an unusual one. He took hold of each one of us and broke us, taking away our pride. Together we talked over things, confessing petty misunderstandings, jealousies, desire for authority – all these sins that stood in the way of being effective in our work and witness.

6   Morrell Swart, *The Call of Africa: The Reformed Church in America Mission in Sub-Sahara, 1948–1998* (Grand Rapids, MI: Eerdmans, 1998), 45.

Even as the Anuaks had opened their hearts so spontaneously and poured out their burdens, so had we, and our hearts became clean and filled with the love of Christ. We were blessed beyond measure. Then, as never before, we were able to serve God because we had come to newness of life in Christ-over and above our assurance of salvation-and could share fully in the joyful experience of rebirth along with our Anuak friends.[7]

As the church among the Anuak grew, so did the American mission team. The American mission established mission stations and planted churches among the southern tribes of Sudan. RCA missionary presence continued to grow and expand from Akobo to Pibor, Nasir, and Leer. From 1948 to 1964, seven RCA missionary couples and four single missionaries actively shared in the pioneer mission work among the Anuak, Murle, and Nuer people groups. These missionaries included Charles Lee and Kitty Crandell, Lillian Huiskens, Paul and Laurel Arnold, LaVerne and Lorraine Sikkema, Bud and Kate Ekster, Arlene Schuiteman, Paul and Winnifred Hostetter, and Roxanne Sarr.

Independence from colonial rule, which was originally widely celebrated, gave rise to pressure and numerous challenges from Islamic government leaders and impacted Christian mission work in the north and south. This resulted in the eventual expulsion of all Christian workers from the country in 1964. Many expelled American missionaries were reassigned to work in Ethiopia. Several RCA missionaries, including Harvey and Lavina Hoekstra, moved across the Akobo river to Pokwo to continue work among the Anuaks in Ethiopia. From 1962 to 1977, RCA missionaries actively worked among the Anuak, Oromo, Daasanech, and other people groups in Ethiopia until all Christian missionaries were expelled by the communist party in 1977.

This resulted in the further expansion of the RCA mission programs to several other countries in Africa. Arlene Schuiteman moved to Zambia at the request of the Churches Medical Association of Zambia to provide leadership in nursing education with the Brethren in Christ Mission.

Initially, Bob and Morrie Swart moved to Kenya and continued working with the Daasanech in Ileret. However, the Kenyan government was not comfortable with this posting. The RCA and the Africa Inland Church (AIC) decided to begin holistic mission work to reach two semi-nomadic unreached people groups, the Pokot and the Orma. The

---

[7] Swart, *The Call of Africa*, 46.

Water development was an important project in almost all of the locations where RCA missionaries served. Bob Swart works on an irrigation system to bring water to another area. New wells and windmills continue to be needed today.

Pokot live in western Kenya near the Ugandan border at Alale, and the Orma live in the Tana River District of eastern Kenya. The RCA agreed to supply missionaries with special skills, while the AIC would make available a pastor or evangelist and some nursing personnel in each area. The Swarts were instrumental in setting up these stations: tending to all of the government and church transactions, choosing a site, clearing the airstrip, providing water, and building temporary housing. Nearing the end of their careers, the Swarts mentored the next generation of pioneer missionaries until their retirement in 1988. They retired as the longest-serving pioneer RCA missionaries in Africa.

The work among the Pokot began in 1980. It experienced some challenges in the early years with the ongoing cattle rustling and raids from the neighboring Ugandan tribe, the Karamoja. Larry and Linda McAuley and Molly Beaver launched and established the evangelistic, educational, agricultural, and medical development programs. At the time of the McAuleys' departure from Alale in 1997, there was one primary school, a firmly established clinic run by Kenyan nationals, and four firmly planted congregations in Alale. Serving for over ten years, Emery and Sharon Blanksma continued the work and were instrumental in transitioning the work fully to indigenous leadership until their departure in 2004. The McAuleys later returned to introduce an asset-based community development model called the Church Community Mobilization Process. This model helps to break the cycle of dependency and helps church leaders and their congregations work together to bring about positive changes for the whole community, bringing hope, self-esteem, and transformation to churches and communities. To date, the Pokot Project has grown to one primary school, several nursery schools, a girls' secondary school, a clinic with a thirty-bed in-patient center, and twenty-four firmly established churches with numerous outreach posts and nearly 8,000 members.

Sue Scheenstra provides medical
assistance to one of the people
groups in Kenya

In 1982, the Swarts moved to live among the Orma, opening three centers, each with a resident missionary family. Paul and Marcia Leemkuil joined them in their efforts to embody the love of Christ in word and deed. When the Leemkuils departed for health reasons and the Swarts retired, three young families—Roger and Sue Scheenstra, Richard and Donna Swart, and Del and Debra Braaksma—continued the work, building solid friendships and earning the trust of the people. Unfortunately, all missionaries were forced to leave the area because of the violent raids of Somali bandits in 1991. Thankfully, at the people's request, the AIC and the RCA reopened the work in the three centers. To date, the work of friendship evangelism, medical work in two locations, agricultural and water development, and primary and secondary education programs continue. A strong Kenyan national worshipping community has been established with the promise of a budding indigenous church.

From 1975 to 1983, RCA missionaries returned to Sudan. Prior to joining the Orma project, Paul and Marcia Leemkuil joined the American mission team in 1977 to work at Doleib Hill. Paul taught agriculture and Marcia served as a nurse. The Sikkemas returned to Malakal working with Mission Aviation Fellowship in 1978. John and Cheryl Busman returned in 1980 to work with the Sudan Council of Churches in agricultural skills development for lay church leadership. In 1982, Jack and Deborah Swart were assigned to the Association of Christian Resource Organizations Serving Sudan (ACROSS), doing construction and Christian education in Pibor and Juba. "While the missionaries were away after 1964, the Holy Spirit continued to be active through the faithful witness of the Sudanese Christians. Leaders trained during the early years had remained faithful to their tasks in the years of crisis. The nine congregations in the area left by the RCA missionaries had become over 150 worshiping centers. Students in the schools were declaring themselves Christians."[8] Unfortunately, in 1983, conflict erupted, and the civil war was renewed. Many people throughout the south suffered displacement, martyrdom, and famine. With about two million internal refugees settling outside of Khartoum in camps, the Spirit of God moved and the church continued to grow as many confessed faith in Jesus Christ. Because of the need for more training of evangelists and pastors, Barbara Kapenga, who worked in Malakal, was assigned to the theological faculty of the Gereif Bible School in Khartoum, developing the curriculum and coordinating the Theological Education by Extension (TEE) program. In 1989, Peter and Patricia Ford, who had served in Oman, were also assigned to Khartoum. Peter taught courses at the Bible school and TEE program, and Patty taught Arabic and worked at the church, providing leadership in Christian education.

There was tremendous need to provide higher-level training for pastors leading to ordination. The vision of the Rev. Dr. William Anderson, a Presbyterian missionary, and the leadership of PCOS came to fruition in the establishment of the institution which came to be known as Nile Theological College. In preparation to better serve this need, the Fords returned to the U.S. for further studies in 1991. Peter obtained a PhD in Islamic studies from Temple University, and Patty earned a degree in Christian education from Princeton Theological Seminary. In 1994, they returned to further the cause of higher Christian education for Sudanese church leaders. Peter succeeded Bill Anderson as the dean of faculty, and Patty was a member of the faculty. The RCA played a vital role in the growth of the Sudanese church via its early pioneering mission work all the way up to the equipping of church leaders at every level, including certificate, diploma, and bachelor's degrees in theology.

Harry and Pat Miersma served in Ethiopia in the 1970s and then became marriage and family therapists on loan to Wycliffe Bible Translators. After some years in Papua New Guinea, they returned to Africa, where they helped establish the Tumaini Counseling Centre in Nairobi, Kenya, which supports missionaries by providing counseling,

---

[8]   Eugene Heideman, "Following the Holy Spirit Through Africa," *Reformed Review* 49, no. 1 (1995).

consulting, and crisis intervention services. While Harry continued working at the center, Pat delved into how to assist both missionaries and national Christians after experiencing the kinds of trauma related to the many wars and other difficult events occurring in African countries as well as in other parts of the world.

Unfortunately, the dawn of the 2000s brought more intense fighting and political instability closer to Khartoum. As a result, Barbara Kapenga was reassigned to work with the Evangelical Church of the Republic of Niger (EERN) at the Dogon Gao Bible School, a certificate- and diploma-level program to equip church leaders who had completed at least the eighth grade. In 2002, she joined RCA missionary Thomas Johnson at the Bible school. Barbara taught Bible, church history, and other courses. Tom taught agricultural and community development courses, providing rural-based evangelists and pastors with solid tent-making skills. In addition,, Tom was instrumental in teaching leadership development courses, creating print and digital Christian education resources, and sharing a number of audio resources to strengthen the fellowship and witness of the church. From 2002 to 2018, Tom worked with EERN and was assigned to a new appointment in Haiti.

In 2007, Jeremy and Susan Beebout joined the EERN team in Niger. Jeremy works in agricultural development, building and construction coordination, and volunteer engagement. Susan is the EERN health director. They have built a guesthouse and two clinics and have implemented a sustainable healthcare model that provides for the most vulnerable and underserved, assisting EERN with outreach to their Muslim neighbors.

In 2002, Peter Ford and family moved to Addis Ababa to assist the Ethiopian Evangelical Church of Mekane Yesus in establishing the Christian Muslim Relations (CMR) program at the Mekane Yesus Seminary (MYS). As founder, Peter developed the curriculum and provided leadership for the entire program, which was dually supported by the RCA and the Evangelical Lutheran Church in America (ELCA). From the first CMR class, two graduates, Masresha Mengiste and Abdi Tadesse Mulat, were identified to pursue master's degree studies and join the CMR faculty. Masresha, supported by the ELCA, completed his studies at Luther Theological Seminary in St. Paul, Minnesota, and Abdi, supported by the RCA, completed his studies at Fuller Theological Seminary. In 2005, Barbara Kapenga joined the theological department faculty at MYS. In 2009, after seven years of firmly establishing the CMR program and mentoring Peter's successors, the Fords moved to Limuru, Kenya, joining the Islam and Christian Muslim Relations master's degree faculty at St. Paul's University. They served there for nearly three years, and Peter later joined the faculty of Near East School of Theology in Beirut, Lebanon.

Peter and Patty's eldest son, David Ford, became a linguist with the Summer Institute of Linguistics (SIL) of Ethiopia in 2011. His work includes the development of orthographies, linguistic data collection, research, and analysis in order to further Bible translation and language development work.

After ten years of contributing to the development of evangelists, pastors, and church leaders in Ethiopia, Barbara Kapenga departed MYS to serve the Church of Central Africa Presbyterian Nkhoma Synod in Malawi and help them build their new university. She became a consultant and faculty member of Josophat Mwale Theological Institute (JMTI) of Nkhoma University, serving from 2016 to the present.

Having previously served in Malawi and Gambia, Rowland and Jane Van Es became faculty members at St. Paul's University in Kenya. Rowland teaches in the faculties of theology and business. Jane teaches in the faculty of social sciences. From 2004 to the present, they have contributed towards the equipping of numerous pastors, evangelists, and servant leaders in Kenya and East Africa.

With the budding peace agreement between northern and southern Sudan in process, RECONCILE International was established in 2004. The January 9–15, 2011, referendum vote was a result of the 2005 Naivasha Peace agreement between the Khartoum central government and the Sudan People's Liberation Army/Movement (SPLA/M). In 2005, jointly appointed RCA/PCUSA missionaries Del and Debra Braaksma joined RECONCILE, Del as the project manager and Debra as the programs manager. From 2005 to 2010, they were instrumental in firmly establishing RECONCILE's programs and base in Yei. Upon the Braaksmas' departure for a new mission assignment in the U.S., Shelvis and Nancy Smith-Mather were also jointly appointed in 2011. Shelvis became the principal of RECONCILE Peace Institute, and Nancy serves as the coordinator of the South Sudan Education and Peace Program. RECONCILE remains at the forefront of peace talks, mediation, and reconciliation and has trained hundreds of church, community, civic, and military leaders in peacebuilding, trauma healing, reconciliation, civic education, and advocacy.

In 2007, the RCA developed a new partnership with the Africa Instituted Church's Maasai Outreach Mission (MOM). MOM's mission is to share the gospel in word and deed by planting indigenous Maasai churches in the most remote villages of Maasailand. Since the inception of the partnership, MOM has grown from 39 churches with 3,000 members to over 130 churches and over 15,000 members. Our partnership in the training of pastoral leaders, water development, food security, and healthcare—coupled with the clear leading of the Holy Spirit—have contributed to this growth.

In South Africa, the RCA has partnered since 1998 with the Uniting Reformed Church of Southern Africa and the Christian Reformed World Relief Committee, in addition to Christ Memorial Church and Maple Avenue Ministries, RCA churches in Holland, Michigan, in the area of diaconal services.[9] Several early mission trips were made to build relationships and dialogue, and together they have worked to address poverty, HIV/AIDS, and economic development projects. One of the important legacies of this relationship is the impact that it had on the progress of the Reformed family of churches towards reconciliation, including the influence it had on the eventual adoption of the Belhar Confession by the RCA. In 2016, the RCA intentionally worked ecumenically with all of the churches in the township of Botshabelo in the Free State. By partnering with Setshabelo Family and Child Services (SFCS), the challenges of orphaned and vulnerable children were addressed via programs of adoption, foster care, family preservation and crisis intervention. SFCS envisions a community where every child thrives in a loving and caring family. Through provision of family-based child welfare services, SFCS unites and strengthens families in the community in partnership with the government, the faith community and other community stakeholders.

In Mozambique, Chad and Dara Vanden Bosch are working with Audio Scripture Ministries (ASM). Since 2010, Chad has served as ASM's Africa director, assisting national partners in facilitating the recording and distribution of audio scriptures devices in the native dialects of Mozambique and other southern Africa countries. As a nurse, Dara serves as the compassionate ministries coordinator, providing a hospice and palliative care program that strives for dignity in death and uses audio scripture materials to comfort hurting patients, family, and friends. Tens of thousands audio scripture devices have been distributed

---

[9]   Additional information regarding the collaboration of the Reformed Church in America with South African organizations was provided by Paul Scholten of Christ Memorial Reformed Church in Holland, Michigan.

and are instrumental in churches' evangelistic, discipleship, and care ministries.

This is a snapshot of the rich history of the RCA mission engagement in Africa, started by Wilma Katts and Robert and Morrie Swart in 1948. Three generations of Swarts have served in Africa from 1948 to 2018. Jack and Debbie Swart served in Sudan and Kenya until his tragic death along with their two sons in a traffic accident near Eldoret, Kenya, in 1989. In 1993, when Dick Swart ended service with AIC and the Orma Project in Kenya, he and his family moved to Ethiopia, and they reopened the church planting work among the Daasanech along the Omo River in partnership with Society in Mission Ethiopia and the Ethiopian Kale Hiwot Church in 1994. Dick's windmill project provided agricultural training, constructed windmills, and utilized them to irrigate crops along the river. As a nurse, Donna provided quality healthcare at the local clinic. In 2008, Caleb and Joanna Swart joined his parents and the Daasanech team, supporting them in the windmill, agricultural, and nursing work. After assisting in the mission with the Daasanech people in Ethiopia, Caleb and Joanna moved to Tanzania in 2015 to work with AIM's Training in Mission Outreach (TIMO).

They contributed to the equipping of the next generation of missionaries, expatriates and indigenous church leaders in Africa. Caleb served as the station manager of TIMO Engedi base, assisting with the setup and training of TIMO mission sites and teams. Joanna provided support to the families of TIMO team members and served as a medical resource to TIMO teams. Having accomplished the Daasanech Project's goal of firmly planting an indigenous church that was self-propagating, self-reproducing, and self-sustaining, Dick and Donna retired from mission service in 2018. This same year, Caleb and Joanna ended their mission service with RCA, discerning a call to another career opportunity.

The primary types of ministries completed by RCA missionaries

The early missionaries focused on developing grammar, syntax, and vocabulary tools in order to devise a script for writing in Anuak and Murle and to teach basic literacy. They focused on Bible translation. The Anuak translation of the New Testament was completed by Harvey Hoekstra. The pastoral team focused on pastoral care, preaching, teaching, and the development of Bible studies and other Christian education resources. The development of indigenous church leadership

The Daasanech Mission Church
in Ethiopia

was a collaborative effort cultivated via weekly Bible study, evangelism, youth, and women's work. Agricultural development work provided food security for the mission station and the community. Working with the village chiefs, bush schools were established to teach basic literacy. Missionaries provided leadership and curriculum development for the mission schools in Akobo, Pibor, and Nasir, and they established a school for girls in Akobo. Missionary nurses worked with the medical teams in rudimentary clinics providing prenatal care, basic healthcare, and health education.

The situation in Africa today

Over seventy years have passed since the Swarts, the Hoekstras, and Wilma Kats arrived in Akobo. Today, the Presbyterian Church of South Sudan (PCOSS) has grown to over 1 million members with 500 congregations and 265 pastors. The Anuak, Murle, Nuer, and other southern people groups have been reached with the gospel. From the mid-1980s to the early 2000's, the RCA supported theological education via Gereif Bible School and Nile Theological College. To date, the RCA continues to partner with PCOSS in leadership development via support of its Theological Education by Extension (TEE) program.

Since gaining independence on July 9, 2011, South Sudan has experienced numerous conflicts that have resulted in civil war. In response to these ongoing challenges, the RCA supports trauma healing, peacebuilding, reconciliation, and community development programs that impact South Sudanese churches and communities via our mission partners RECONCILE International and ACROSS. The RCA continues to support the growth of South Sudanese churches and their role in advocating for lasting peace and nation-building.

Overall, RCA mission efforts have expanded to seven countries in Africa, including South Sudan, Ethiopia, Kenya, Malawi, Mozambique, South Africa, and Niger. The RCA currently works with fifteen mission partners and thirty missionaries and mission partner personnel.

RCA Global Mission remains directly engaged in church planting and pioneering holistic mission work among unreached and under-reached people groups in Africa. The RCA is actively involved in Bible translation, dissemination of audio bibles, leadership development, child welfare, and sustainable community development. In 1960, there were approximately 30 million Christians in sub-Saharan Africa; today, there are over 550 million. This tremendous growth warrants and demands significant assistance in the area of theological education to effectively and responsibly equip the church in Africa. The RCA praises God for the privilege and opportunity to share in Christ's mission and the growth and development of the church in Africa.

For further reading

Barker, Jeff Allen with Arlene Schuitema. *Sioux Center Sudan: A Missionary Nurse's Journey*. Peabody, MA: Hendrickson Publishers, 2018.

Barker, Jeff. *Iowa Ethiopia: A Missionary Nurse's Journey Continues*. Peabody, MA: Hendrickson Publishers, 2019.

Cogswell, James A. *No Turning Back: A History of American Presbyterian Involvement in Sub-Saharan Africa 1833–2000*. Philadelphia: Xlibris Corporation, 2007.

Heideman, Eugene P. "Following the Holy Spirit Through Africa." *Reformed Review* 49, no. 1 (1995).

Hoekstra, Harvey T. *From "Knotted Strings" to Talking Bibles* (originally published as *"Honey, We're Going to Africa!"*). Pasadena, CA: William Carey Library, 2003.

Swart, Morrell. *The Call of Africa: The Reformed Church in America Mission in Sub-Sahara, 1948–1998*. Grand Rapids, MI: Eerdmans, 1998.

CHAPTER 11

Taiwan—1950

Jeanette Beagley-Koolhaas and Alan Beagley

Taiwan is a small island 100 miles off the coast of mainland China. Shaped like a tobacco leaf, it is about the size of New Jersey: 80 miles wide and 150 miles long. The eastern two-thirds of the island is mountainous and sparsely inhabited. The western third is where most of the 23 million people live. Traveling from east to west across the island by bus or car is difficult; the 80-mile journey along mountainous, twisting, narrow roads can take as much as eight hours. Traveling between north and south on the west side of the country, however, one can drive along a modern freeway or ride a Japanese-style "bullet" train that takes only about an hour and a half. The eastern side of the country is less developed, so transportation is more challenging. There are domestic airline services from city to city.

Taiwan has been ruled by many nations, and today it has a great desire to be recognized as an independent nation. At one time, it was ruled by the Netherlands, and there is still a place called Zeelandia in memory of those days. The Portuguese named the island *Ilha Formosa*, meaning "beautiful island," and for a long time "Formosa" was the name by which the island was known.

Taiwan was ceded to Japan in 1895 following a war between China and Japan, but soon after the defeat of Japan at the end of World War II, the Chinese Nationalists (under Chiang Kai-Shek and his party), fleeing the Communist takeover of the Chinese mainland, took over Taiwan and established martial law. They used great force to suppress dissent, killing thousands, including many academics and many leaders of the Presbyterian Church of Taiwan (PCT). The PCT was targeted because the church's large membership made it the most influential organization on the island and a threat to the Nationalist Party.

Taiwan's population is made up of the long-time Taiwanese occupants of the island who originally came from the Fujian Province in China, "Mainlanders" who came from China with Nationalist leader Chiang Kai-sheik, and sixteen or more indigenous tribes that each speak their own languages. There is an effort today to revive the use of those indigenous languages to help guard against their dying out altogether. Taiwanese (a version of the Fujianese dialect spoken in parts of the Chinese mainland) is the mother tongue of many of the people, but when the Nationalists took over the island, they decreed that Mandarin would be the official language.

Early missionary activity in Taiwan

Early mission work in Taiwan was begun by missionaries from England and Scotland who worked mainly in the southern part of the island. One early leader was James Maxwell, an English medical doctor who arrived in 1865. He was joined by William Campbell and Thomas Barclay. George Leslie Mackay, a missionary from Canada, served in Tamsui in the northern part of the island, devoting himself to medical work, education, and planting churches. Today, there is a statue of Mackay in Tamsui in recognition of his work. A large hospital and nursing school, the fruit of his labors, now have locations in Taipei as well. In addition to founding elementary and secondary schools, the missionaries established three colleges/seminaries in Taipei (in the north), Tainan (in the south), and Yushan (on the east coast).

RCA missionaries come to Taiwan

Many of the missionaries who came to Taiwan in the 1940s had originally gone to China, where some had served for twenty or more years and then were forced out by the Communist regime. Among these were the RCA missionaries Jeanne Walvoord and Ruth Broekema. The predominant language in the Presbyterian Church was Taiwanese, but any missionary working in schools had to use Mandarin Chinese, which was the language mandated by the Nationalist government.

The RCA missionaries did not seek to establish separate "Reformed" congregations but instead worked in partnership with the Presbyterian Church of Taiwan (PCT), as did missionaries from many different countries and denominations in the early years. There were missionaries from England, Scotland, Wales, Canada, the United States, Korea, India, and Japan assisting the PCT in its work and under its direction.

The RCA emphasized the importance of learning the local language to better understand the local people and culture. The Schroeders, Noordhoffs, and Bill Estell and his first wife Eileen all learned Taiwanese when they arrived in Taiwan. Later on, missionaries working in educational institutions were expected to use Mandarin in the classroom, even if the other teachers and students used Taiwanese among themselves. In the Presbyterian Church seminaries, however, the main language was Taiwanese, and many students resisted speaking Mandarin, which they viewed to a large extent as the language of the "foreign" mainland invaders. An exception was Yushan Theological College and Seminary in Hualien on the East Coast, which primarily served the indigenous Christian churches. Far more Mandarin was used at Yushan than at the other institutions, because Mandarin was the only language that the indigenous students had in common.

Early missionaries translated the Bible and many hymns into Taiwanese using a romanized representation of the language rather than Chinese characters. These continued to be used in the Presbyterian Church despite the objections of the Nationalist government. Some other Christian bodies in Taiwan used Bibles and hymnals in Mandarin, written in traditional Chinese characters.

Primary ministries completed by RCA missionaries

During the early years of RCA presence in Taiwan, missionaries were actively involved in medical work in the Christian hospitals that had been established in Taiwan. The value of their work was recognized and valued by the general population. As an example of this, one summer a volunteer teacher needed medical attention. The young lady was uncomfortable about seeing a local doctor, so she was taken to a branch of Mackay hospital. She was still somewhat apprehensive, but then she read the plaque on the wall. She came back with a smile

Students from the indigenous
tribes of the East Coast
lead worship at the Yushan
Theological College and
Seminary in Hualien

because the plaque read, "This hospital was built with donations from the Reformed Church in America." Dr. Samuel and Lucille Noordhoff worked in the medical field. Sam became a world-renowned plastic surgeon specializing in the repair of cleft palates and teaching many of his students to do this work. Today, Taiwan is still well known as a center for cleft-palate surgery. As Dr. Noordhoff often said, "We come to work ourselves out of a job"—a good motto for all missionaries.

Some missionaries came to work with the University Student Centers that were established by the Presbyterian Church close to universities and colleges in major cities. Some of this work involved teaching English, which also became a way to build personal relationships with students and share their faith. In addition to learning English, many college students were open to learning about the church and biblical teaching. The PCT began its Summer English Program, which brought many RCA members to Taiwan for a summer or a year to teach English. Local college students would attend for five to six weeks in the summer to study at an English camp in one of the major cities. They were required to speak English all day long, which improved their conversational English and supplemented the more academic English they encountered in textbooks or other study materials.

Some of the RCA volunteers who came just for the summer decided to stay for a year or two, teaching English in local schools and building relationships not only with their students but also with the Presbyterian Church. Some of those teachers returned home initially but later came back to Taiwan as full-time missionaries. Examples are David and Charlene Alexander and Jeanette Koolhaas (now Beagley-Koolhaas). A significant number of RCA ministers and church members spent a summer or a year as English teachers in Taiwan. One summer, there were two Smiths in the group: Harry Smith, who went on to

Taiwanese college students attended the Summer English Program
to improve their English. Teacher Jeanette Koolhaas is located
in the front row, second from left.

become a noted CBS newscaster, and Paul Smith, who later became the director of the library at Western Theological Seminary.

In addition to teaching English, RCA missionaries taught in Christian schools and theological seminaries in multiple regions of the country. Subjects frequently taught included English, Bible, theology, evangelism, and music. Administrative assistance was also provided in English to seminary presidents. Judy Estell, Bill Estell's second wife, was invited to teach English in a maximum-security prison in the Hualien region. She agreed to do so if she could teach the Bible in English. This led to her giving English Bible lessons to men in prison twice a week for over twenty-five years.

The Presbyterian Church was viewed with suspicion by the Nationalist government because of its public statements concerning human rights and opposing martial law. The volunteer English teachers were also watched closely and knew that at least one student in every class would be reporting to the government what they said and did. The security services read, and even microfilmed, incoming and outgoing mail, and they listened in on phone calls. Some full-time missionaries were blacklisted because they spoke out in agreement with the PCT views on human rights and other issues. Some were refused visas to return for an additional term. RCA missionaries Wendell and Joyce Karsen relocated to Hong Kong, and Roland and Judy Van Es to the Philippines. Even some citizens who had left to study overseas were denied permission to return, some for as long as forty years without being able to visit their homes and families. It is only in recent years,

RCA missionaries attend a Presbyterian Church of Taiwan mission conference: (*l. to r.*) Bill and Judy Estell, Jeanette and Alan Beagley-Koolhaas, Barbara Wyma, and Char and David Alexander

with a change of government, that many of those former exiles have been officially exonerated.

In the 1980s, Dr. C. M. Kao, the general secretary of the Presbyterian Church of Taiwan, was imprisoned for many years because of the church's stance on human rights. Churches around the world wrote letters supporting him and urging the government to release him. He could have been released sooner if he had agreed to leave the country, but he insisted that his rights as a Taiwanese citizen be recognized. Anyone interested in the work of the PCT on human rights can read volume one of Wendell Karsen's book *The Church Under the Cross* (particularly chapter two).

The situation today in Taiwan

As a missionary in Taiwan, I often traveled by taxi. One day, a driver asked what I was doing in Taiwan. Hearing that I was an English teacher, he assumed that I was making a good salary teaching in one of the schools for intensive English learning. On hearing that I was a missionary working with the PCT, he remarked, "They care about the people of this island." The Presbyterian Church continues to be held in high regard today.

Today, 5 percent of Taiwan's population is Christian, half Protestant and half Catholic. As of today, there are no full-time RCA missionaries in Taiwan. The last couple, David and Charlene Alexander, retired in 2018, but the RCA and Presbyterian Church in Taiwan continue to be partners. The PCT has enough of its own teachers and doctors and does not need as many missionaries. Some churches still send missionaries to Taiwan, but the number has declined. Both the PCT and the RCA are members of the World Communion of Reformed Churches and the World Council of Churches. Some of the PCT's ministers and professors undertake further studies at an RCA seminary and then return to Taiwan to teach in the seminaries. Today, there are Taiwanese RCA congregations in various parts of the United States (including at least one that uses the name "Formosa"). Some of these have services in Mandarin and more recently also in English for their young people who are not proficient in the Taiwanese language.

The Presbyterian Church in Taiwan continues to be a strong church in the country, known for its emphasis in support of human rights and a democratic government. In response to requests from the Presbyterian Church in Taiwan, the RCA provides funds to help in seminary education, evangelism among unreached indigenous peoples, disaster relief, and programs of the Presbyterian Church such as the Fisherman's Service Center and the Rainbow Project, which serves young girls who have been trapped in prostitution. The Reformed Church in America stands beside it as a supportive partner, buoyed by the many years of working together for the growth of God's kingdom in Taiwan.

In addition to requesting mission coworkers and resources, the PCT seeks the support of its partners in North America and Europe with other issues that face the church. The PCT has encouraged American churches to support Taiwan's acceptance into the United Nations, and strongly supports the independence of Taiwan. It asks its ecumenical partners to stand in solidarity with the church in the endeavor to obtain Chinese recognition of Taiwan's sovereignty.

For further reading

Karsen, Wendell Paul. *The Church under the Cross: Mission in Asia in Times of Turmoil: A Missionary Memoir.* 2 volumes. The Historical Series of the Reformed Church in America. Grand Rapids, MI: Eerdmans, 2010 and 2012.

Mackay, George Leslie. *From Far Formosa: The Island, its People and Missions.* Grand Rapids, MI: Fleming H. Revell, 1895. Republished as *From Far Formosa.* Dayton, OH: Cave Book Store, 1965.

CHAPTER 12

Europe—1994

Richard Otterness

Origins of Protestant Christianity in central and eastern Europe

The ancient roots of Christianity in Europe can be traced back to the account in chapter 16 of the book of Acts. A man from Macedonia urges Paul, in a vision, to "come over to Macedonia," that is, to what we know today as a region in southern Europe. Over time, Christianity spread from Macedonia deeper into the continent.

Long before the sixteenth-century Protestant Reformation, a merchant from Lyon named Peter Waldo founded the Poor of Lyon in the 1170s. Known as the Waldensians, the group's focus included preaching the Word in the streets and making texts from the Bible available in the local languages.[1] This movement suffered years of persecution as a precursor of the Protestant movement in Italy. The Waldensian Church continues to bear a vital witness some 800 years

---

[1]   The Waldensians, known as "Valdese" in Italy, describe the origins of this movement in a document from Carcassonne, France, that details the beginnings of this group "by a certain citizen of Lyon by the name of Valdesius" (Giorgio Tourn, *You Are My Witnesses: The Waldensians Across 800 Years* [Torino, Italy: Claudiana Editrice, 1989], 11). He is popularly known today as Peter Waldo.

later with 120 congregations, and the Reformed Church in America (RCA) has contributed to Waldensian pastoral work, refugee ministry, and volunteer service. Other groups also foreshadowed what would become the Protestant Reformation, including John Wycliffe in the mid-fourteenth century and Jan Hus in the early fifteenth century.

The Protestant Reformation in the sixteenth century was a watershed movement. North Americans with a cursory knowledge may associate it with places like Wittenberg and Augsburg or Strasburg and Geneva. What appears to be less known is the story of the Protestant Reformation in central and eastern Europe.

Some believers, moved by John Calvin's charge to spread the gospel across the continent, made their way to countries including Poland, Estonia, and Hungary. In the Hungarian city of Debrecen (the "Geneva of the East"), the Hungarian Reformed Church established a college in 1538 and a publishing house in 1561.

How and with whom the RCA first got involved

The Reformed Church in America became involved in Europe in a variety of ways before any full-time, resident missionaries were sent. For a short time, the RCA supported non-RCA mission workers in Marseille, France; Greece; and Warsaw, Poland. More recently, the RCA continued this practice in Italy and Hungary.

In Russia, the RCA joined a new partnership formed by the National Council of Churches of Christ to establish Christian witness in Moscow with four other ecumenical partners. The mission focused on outreach to expatriates, especially those from Africa, providing social support, practical services, fellowship, and worship. Today, this ministry involves people from almost 30 nations.

In Slovakia, through the RCA's Adventures in Mission (AIM) initiative in the 1990s, short-term young adult volunteers taught English to youth in the city of Kosice. Years later, RCA missionaries would provide pastoral support in Kosice to longer-term young adult volunteers teaching English, working with church youth groups, and serving as resident mentors in halfway houses for young women who came out of orphanages.

During the communist era, professor Eugene Osterhaven of Western Theological Seminary responded with great concern for the Reformed church in Hungary. Seminaries and churches had been closed or greatly restricted in their activities. Pastors were trained at Reformed bishops' kitchen tables in parts of Hungary and Ukraine. The renowned library at the Reformed seminary in Sarospatak, Hungary, was gutted of its fine collection. After the fall of communism in 1989, Dr. Osterhaven spearheaded a rigorous campaign with RCA congregations and others that resulted in the donation of books and funds to reestablish the Sarospatak seminary and its library. Subsequently, Dr. Osterhaven was welcomed warmly as a guest lecturer in theology at the seminary.

In 1994, the General Synod committed the RCA to sending full-time missionaries to eastern Europe. The first missionaries were Dave and Joy Zomer, who were sent to Hungary, and Jim and Beth Harrison, who went to Estonia.

Hungary is a mostly rural country of approximately 10 million people, with around 2 million living in the capital city of Budapest. Located in the geographic center of Europe, the country was challenged in 1995 by the transition from communism to democracy and the cultural shift from being an eastern European country to being part of more progressive central Europe. When the RCA approached Bishop Toth of the Reformed Church in Hungary (RCH) about a partnership, the bishop suggested it would be good for someone to teach English at the Károly Gáspár Református University (KGRU) in Budapest. This university is home to one of the four theological seminaries of the RCH. Thus, teaching became David Zomer's first task. Initially teaching American studies courses and forming an active student fellowship group at the university, the Zomers focused on learning the unique Hungarian, or Magyar, language. Soon, they were able to develop new opportunities for ministry, including mission and work groups, year-long exchange opportunities for RCA and Hungarian Reformed members, and further KGRU student involvement.

The Zomers' work in Hungary developed significant relationships with a number of Hungarian Reformed pastors, offering friendship, support, and encouragement. Pastors were stretched to a breaking point, sometimes serving three to five congregations at once. Reaching people conditioned by atheism during communist times presented new pastoral challenges, as did the pressure to return the church to its pre-communist days. To have the support of an RCA mission partner was important and beneficial to them in their personal lives and in their vocations.

The other early endeavor in Europe was with Jim and Beth Harrison and their family in the northern European nation of Estonia. The Republic of Estonia is one of the three Baltic states in northeastern Europe, the others being Latvia and Lithuania. Unlike landlocked

Hungary, Estonia is surrounded by water on three sides, and to the east by Russia. With a population of only 1.33 million people, this small country became a constituent part of the USSR in 1940. When Estonia declared its independence in 1991, it was a poor nation. However, the country transitioned smoothly and quickly into a parliamentary democracy with one of the fastest-growing market economies in Europe.

In 1995, the Harrison family moved to Estonia, where they would live and work for the next thirteen years. They partnered with United World Missions, an organization committed to church planting across eastern Europe. They would eventually also work with the Evangelical Christian and Baptist Union and some Pentecostal churches. The vision was to plant a church with Estonians in such a way that Estonians would want to duplicate the project in other communities. This would not be easy; the Harrisons found that many Estonians who were coming out of a communist context saw Christianity as something imported from the outside.

The strategy was to develop a cell church in the city of Tartu, based on biblical teaching and fellowship in small group settings. After much work, the church saw thirty to thirty-five new believers in Christ. While Estonia was the Harrisons' main focus, they also traveled to the other Baltic nations, supporting Christian leaders and church planters. This has been typical of RCA mission workers in Europe: living and working primarily in one country while also developing relationships and projects in neighboring countries.

The primary types of ministries performed by RCA missionaries

In her paper "A Protestant Perspective on Mission in Eastern and Central Europe" missiologist Anne-Marie Kool cites Croatian professor Davor Peterlin, who "observes that Western Christians often operate with the false assumption that 'the period of Communist rule in the former Eastern European countries has totally annihilated Christian witness,' and they think that what is needed is 'not only sporadic church-planting, but the actual creation of Christian culture *ex nihilo.*' Peterlin states that in fact the contrary is true, 'the countries in question are today at least as Christian as most Western countries, if indeed not more Christian.'"[2]

---

[2]   Anne-Marie Kool, "A Protestant Perspective on Mission in Eastern and Central Europe" *Occasional Papers on Religion in Eastern Europe* 20, no. 6 (2000). Kool cites Davor Peterlin, "The Wrong Kind of Missionary: A Semi-Autobiographic Outcry," *Mission Studies* 12, no. 2 (1995): 167.

The Zomers (*at left*) hosted many work crews from RCA churches
to help update the Ecumene property in Italy

Most RCA missionaries in Europe shared Peterlin's view. They developed relationships with vibrant European churches, Christian organizations, and individuals. Having emerged from what some would say has been the heart of old Christendom into the new, exciting, and uncertain time some call "post-Christendom," European Christians and churches have much they could teach Westerners about Christian life and witness in changing times. In this context, RCA missionaries in Europe have come to see their role as companions, sharing the journey with indigenous Christians in missional activities from evangelism to the pursuit of social justice. As RCA Global Mission describes it, RCA mission philosophy in Europe has included

- · A commitment to partnerships
- · The priority of relationships
- · A commitment to long-term mission
- · A willingness to invest in mission personnel
- · Mission that reflects the gospel's bias to care for the marginalized
- · Mission that is holistic
- · A willingness to embrace innovations
- · The importance of ecumenism in Reformed mission

Following the Zomers and the Harrisons, other RCA missionaries went to Europe committed to these principles. While the Harrisons moved on to Bahrain, the Zomers continued in Europe but moved to Italy. Other new missionaries included Jack and Susan Dabney in Albania, Eric and Nancy Titus in Croatia, Dick and Carolyn Otterness in Hungary, JJ and Tim Ten Clay in Italy, and Jeff and Chelsea Lampen in Romania. One of the primary types of mission work in Europe became working for justice in the spirit of Micah 6:8: "What does the Lord require of you but to do justice, and to love kindness, and to walk humbly with your God?" The intentional work for justice and reconciliation was developed especially in Italy and in Hungary. In the early 2000s, the RCA's work in Europe focused on justice, reconciliation, and walking alongside the mission partners to strengthen their leadership and pastoral support.

The Zomers' move to Italy marked a new relationship with the Methodist and the Evangelical Waldensian Churches. These small Protestant churches in a Roman Catholic country demonstrated a strong commitment to mission. Italy was a new field for the RCA, and the work there began with Dave Zomer assisting on justice publications for the Waldensian moderator's office in Rome, as well as working with Italian Methodists and RCA work groups to upgrade the Ecumene retreat center in Veletri south of Rome. After completing the work at Ecumene, Dave and Joy were invited to serve in Pachino and Scicli, two congregations in southern Sicily.

Dave served as the pastor of both churches, one Waldensian and one Methodist, while also acting as director of the church preschool; Joy worked with youth in the churches and ran ESL classes; and together they helped the local congregation develop an immigrant receiving center in Scicli. Over time, the mission with refugees became more extensive, and a special focus was on helping migrant women get the spiritual, emotional, and practical support they needed to survive and thrive in Italy. After David Zomer returned to pastoral work in North America, JJ Ten Clay and her husband moved to Palermo, Sicily, and continued the partnership with the Waldensians. Their work centered on justice and reconciliation for immigrants while also serving in a church community.

In Hungary, the Otternesses partnered with the Reformed Church in Hungary's (RCH) mission office and ecumenical office. The RCH is the dominant Protestant church in Hungary, with 1200 congregations in a nation the size of Indiana. The Roma (pejoratively called "gypsies") are the largest ethnic minority in Hungary and in Europe. They are despised and are often the object of hate speech and

The sixth annual national gathering of Roma in
eastern Hungary in 2015, an outcome of
the national strategy that the Otternesses
helped initiate

hate campaigns by majority populations. In many Roma communities the poverty is great, though not all Roma are poor. While some RCH congregations developed relationships with neighboring Roma, most congregations and the RCH denomination were not involved with the marginal population living on the outskirts of two-thirds of the nation's communities. The initial charge for the RCA missionaries was to work with the RCH in developing a rationale and strategy for comprehensive, holistic Roma mission nation-wide. This action plan was developed successfully and is now implemented entirely by the Roma and the Hungarians.

Tangentially, the Otternesses provided leadership and coordination for an international young adult volunteer network that put Roma and non-Roma in year-long service in countries across Europe. First called Roma-Gadje Dialogue Through Service (RGDTS), its purpose was to create opportunities for informal education, dialogue, and engagement in order to challenge stereotypes and racism. Churches, including the Waldensians, participated as partners. Some RCA volunteers participated, many of whom found church-related vocations when they returned to the U.S.

The mission work in Hungary expanded to include health education as part of Christian community development projects. Perhaps the most significant ministry, however, was an intense reconciliation ministry called "Healing the Wounds of Ethnic Conflict."

Carolyn Otterness provided training and leadership in this movement in Ukraine. Her work included education and awareness training on matters of racism, prejudice, and the healing that comes through the cross of Christ.

In Albania, a nation in the southern Balkans where the majority are at least nominally Muslim and where many Roma live, the RCA mission for justice was important. Susan Dabney walked among the poorest of the poor (Roma) in the capital city's huge garbage dump, offering what food or other help she could. She also visited inmates in the women's prison, along with patients and their families at the Mother Theresa Hospital.

In addition to the pursuit of justice, a second type of missional priority in Europe has been to walk alongside missional partners and encourage their development in theological education and pastoral support. This was the primary task in Albania. Christian pastors often have only a high-school education or less. The Dabneys mentored pastors informally, and Jack Dabney taught at several pastoral training schools, as well as holding faculty positions at the Albanian Bible Institute and the Evangelical Theological College. The mission also included home Bible studies with Albanians and leading the Upper Room retreat center for pastors, church leaders, and missionaries. The Albanian Evangelical Alliance, representing 150 evangelical churches and Christian organizations, has been the partner for this work. The churches are young, having been established since the fall of communism in Albania in 1990.

Theological education was also a priority in Osijek, Croatia. Eric and Nancy Titus served on the faculty of the Evangelical Theological Seminary there until 2012. Because students came from different Balkan countries with different languages, much of the teaching took place in English. Nancy tutored students and taught English classes. Eric served as professor of theology and offered informal pastoral support to students and colleagues. He also served as an assistant to the Hungarian Reformed Croatian bishop, particularly in ecumenical relationships.

The context of northern Croatia made life and work there challenging. Osijek showed signs of the damage done during the Croatian War of Independence, fought from 1991 to 1995 between Croatia—which had declared independence from the Socialist Federal Republic of Yugoslavia—and Serb-controlled Yugoslavian forces. Croatia succeeded in gaining autonomous statehood, but at great price. Many survivors of

Roma children with Richard Otterness at a Christian summer camp in Hungary in 2015

the war could be characterized by mistrust, fatalism, and violence just below the surface that could erupt if scratched. Croatia was a difficult place to do mission, though the need was and remains great.

In Romania, the Lampens joined the work of the New Horizons Foundation in the city of Lupeni, located in the southern Carpathian Alps. The Jui Valley, in which Lupeni is located, is one of the poorest regions in Romania. The unemployment rate exceeds 50 percent in the area. Where coal mining was once the dominant industry, now abandoned industrial structures mar the landscape of an otherwise beautiful area.

Jeff Lampen had been introduced to foreign mission firsthand as a year-long volunteer in Hungary. Chelsea Lampen had enjoyed short-term volunteer experience in Romania. Both Western Theological Seminary graduates, together they heard the call to go to Romania. In Lupeni, the RCA involvement has been largely in facilitating IMPACT, a program providing experiences for youth in developing teamwork and leadership skills that they are encouraged to take back home. IMPACT clubs typically meet once or twice a week and work through a multi-year curriculum of activities. Meanwhile, RCA missionaries have been creating a faith-based curriculum to reinforce the themes of the IMPACT program. They have also facilitated a partnership with Northwestern College, offering a study-abroad program.

The situation in Europe today

Europe is going through a time of major transition. Ultra-right-wing sentiments are growing and manifest themselves in government elections and in a rise of hate speech and sometimes violence. The apparent cohesion once offered by the European Union may be fracturing. As with other church and Christian organizations, mission happens in a variety of ways, and some of them are unhelpful and even hurtful. Locals speak of "hit and run" mission, where foreigners come in, quickly assess a situation, develop and implement a project plan with minimal or no consultation with locals, do the project *for* (not *with*) local people, then disappear never to be seen again. Relationships are not important in that type of work. Parachurch organizations often operate without accountability and without interest in cooperating with, or learning from, long-term mission personnel from established churches. Money is not always helpful, sometimes creating an unhealthy dependence that benefits no one in the long run. The RCA's mission philosophy, which has served as the foundation of work in Europe, is still needed.

The important work in Lupeni, Romania, continues with the efforts of a young couple, Felipe and Janelle de Waard-Silva. Along with the New Horizons Foundation, the de Waard-Silvas have a special concern for what is known as the Dallas community in that area. Poverty amongst Roma and others is extreme. In addition to youth work, a church is also being planted in the Dallas community in Romania.

Another couple, Doug and Diane McClintic, have been dividing their time between the U.S. and Hungary, working with leadership development and church-planting efforts in the Debrecen area, and building bridges with North American congregations, classes, synods, and other groups in the RCA. In 2020, they plan to move permanently to Debrecen, Hungary, to have a full-time mission presence there.

With the pressures and tensions in Europe, with a growing post-secular young population where many are looking for something secular values and materialism doesn't provide, where refugees continue to come to European shores, and where xenophobia and racism are on the rise, the opportunities and need for Christ's work and signs of Christ's presence is greater than ever.

Editors' update

Very recent mission activity has located an RCA family in the Netherlands where many Kurdish people have relocated. They will partner with Operation Mobilization to share the gospel with their Muslim neighbors through proclamation, relationship, and community involvement. Another couple has been sent to Turkey, working on

Christian radio and TV programming, mentoring new believers, preaching and teaching, and providing counseling services for regional sending organizations. New partnership relationships in Europe are being sought and developed whenever the opportunities arise.

For further reading

Frederick, Kevin E. *With Their Backs Against the Mountain: 850 Years of Waldensian Witness,* North Charleston, SC: CreateSpace Independent Publishing Platform, 2018.

Kool, Anne-Mary, "Revolutions in European Mission: What Has Been Achieved in 25 Years of Eastern European Mission?" In *Mission in Central and Eastern Europe: Realities, Perspectives, Trends,* edited by Corneliu Constantineau, Marcel Marcelaru, Anne-Marie Kool, and Mihai Himcinschi. Oxford: Regnujm Books International, 2016.

Kool, Anne-Marie. *God Moves in a Mysterious Way: The Hungarian Protestant Foreign Mission Movement (1756–1951).* PhD diss. Utrecht University, 1993. (Available at researchgate.net).

Tourn, Giorgio. *You Are My Witnesses: The Waldensians Across 800 Years.* Torino, Italy: Claudiana Editrice, 1989.

People against Poverty. "Life in Dallas - Romania." YouTube video. November 17, 2015.

CHAPTER 13

Four Characteristics of RCA Global Mission

Charles E. Van Engen

Introduction

In the chapters of this book, we have met a "cloud of witnesses" very much like what the author of Hebrews wanted us to see with regard to persons in the Old Testament whose lives God used in God's mission in the world. We often call these people "heroes of the faith." The author of Hebrews does not call them "heroes." Rather, they are presented as ordinary people through whom God did extraordinary things. In fact, the author of Hebrews calls them "aliens and strangers on earth" (Hebrews 11:13). Their common characteristic was their faith in God's provision and action. Through their faith, their "weakness was turned to strength" (11:34). Many of them experienced great suffering (11:35-38). Moreover, amazingly, the author of Hebrews tells us that "God had planned something better for us so that only together with us would they be made perfect" (11:40). The "us" in this passage are the readers of the book of Hebrews, then and now, including RCA mission folks during the past 180 years, as well as you and me today.

God's mission happens in specific times and places, but it extends over centuries. When Luke wrote the book of Acts, he wanted his readers to understand that. So the book of Acts has no ending. It simply stops with Luke telling us that, "Paul stayed [in Rome] in his own rented house and welcomed all who came to see him. Boldly and without hindrance he preached the kingdom of God and taught about the Lord Jesus Christ" (Acts 28:30-31). The Holy Spirit is still writing the book of Acts, and some of that mission activity of the Holy Spirit flowed through the "cloud of witnesses" to which the chapters of this book have pointed.

As I read the various chapters of this book, I was again amazed, inspired, encouraged, and challenged by the stories of ordinary people through whom God did extraordinary things that impact the church and world even today. As I listened to those stories, several recurring themes about RCA Global Mission kept calling my attention. In this final chapter, I want to mention four themes or characteristics of RCA intercultural mission that these stories have in common. In my mind, these four themes come together in a metaphor of a marathon race. God's mission down through the centuries has been like a marathon race. The Apostle Paul likened his own missionary journey to a race (2 Timothy 4:7, Galatians 2:2).

Picture a marathon race. It is early morning in some city in the world. The street is packed with hundreds of runners, as far up the street as you can see. The race marshal has his starting gun pointed to the sky. Women and men from all over the world are preparing to begin their run. But this marathon is a little different. Each runner has been asked to affix a set of starting blocks to the pavement.

"Runners in position," the marshal calls out.

Hundreds of runners bend down, put their feet in the starting blocks, lean with their knuckles on the ground, straining, ready to leap forward to begin their race. The starting gun sounds. The runners jump up. The "cloud of witnesses" is running past you. The race is on.

RCA Global Mission is historical

The marathon begins in the starting blocks. None of us participates in God's mission in a vacuum. God has prepared the way. Others have run this race before us. Today, no matter where you and I go in the world, even among groups that some would call unreached, there are and have been followers of Jesus in that area or country long before we arrived. And the peoples of those cultures to which we may be sent already know something about God. As the early European missionaries discovered when they went to Africa, the Africans did not yet know God's grace and salvation in Jesus Christ, but they knew much about God, creator of heaven and earth. In addition, today's intercultural missionaries everywhere in the world often discover that other Christian missionaries have been there long before they arrived.

So when we place our feet in the starting blocks of RCA Global Mission, it is important for us to learn about, learn from, and thoughtfully engage with the past. An appreciation of our global mission heritage provides us the starting blocks, the springboards to missionary action today and tomorrow. When you and I participate in RCA Global Mission, we are part of this history, part of a story that goes back decades and maybe centuries. We get dressed for the race. And as we put our feet in the starting blocks of RCA Global Mission, we join others from all over the world whom God has used to touch the lives of thousands around the globe. We have much to learn from both the triumphs and the mistakes of those who have run the race before us. Many of those folks may not have been RCA personnel, but they may have been our mission partners, or they may have been part of other expressions of Christ's church.

This historical sense of RCA Global Mission is not nostalgia, not a wishful desire to return to an imaginary, wonderful past. First, it was not so wonderful. All over the world we can find the tombstones of missionaries and many of their children who died in the midst of their cross-cultural ministries. Secondly, doing mission a century ago, or even twenty years ago, was very different than doing mission today and tomorrow. The world has changed, cultures and people have changed, and the global church has changed. Even so, when we place our feet in those starting blocks, we are connecting with other ordinary women and men whom God used to do quite extraordinary things in the world of their day. And they invite, inspire, and challenge us to run the race with them. Like good marathon runners, we have been training for this over the past months and years. In terms of the RCA Global Mission marathon, we have been training for this for the past 184 years, ever since the first RCA missionaries went to India.

As we place our feet in those starting blocks of the RCA's mission history, we discover that the RCA has long, historic friendships and partnerships with peoples, churches, and institutions all over the world. We do not begin our missionary activities from scratch. In the Middle East, for example, folks remark that the RCA missionary personnel (like the Zwemers and the Cantines) were there "before petroleum," the discovery of which forever changed the Middle East. We build on the past relationships that those who have gone before us had with mission partner churches, institutions, and governments. With both positive and negative aspects of that past, those relationships continue to impact our present and future mission endeavors. As we have learned in the chapters of this book, RCA Global Mission is firmly grounded in its historic mission practice and presence around the world.

RCA Global Mission is relational

We are off and running our mission marathon. As we run, we look around us to see who else is running with us. And this is really amazing! There are people from so many nations running alongside us in God's mission. There are the Africans, led by the Kenyans, Ethiopians, and Nigerians. There are the Latin Americans: Mexicans, Central Americans, Peruvians, and Brazilians. And there are the Asians: Koreans, Japanese, Taiwanese, Filipinos, Chinese, Thai, and Indonesians. Soon the Chinese church will join in this massive missionary movement to the whole earth. In fact, in the global missionary movement in this new century, the churches in the South and East of the globe are now sending and supporting more full time cross-cultural, international missionaries than the total being sent from Europe and North America combined.

Over 60 percent of all world Christianity is now in Asia, Africa, Latin America, and Oceania. Christianity is no longer a Western religion. This should not surprise us. It was not originally a Western religion. It was originally Middle Eastern, north African, and Asian. And now, in this new century, the missionary endeavor of world evangelization is being carried out as much by churches and missionary agencies from the South and East as it is by those in Europe and North America. In India alone, although the church is a very small minority of the total population, there are over 400 Indian Christian missionary agencies sending missionaries everywhere in the world. In Latin America, more than 600 cross-cultural missionary agencies send and support over 9000 full-time missionaries around the world. South Korea is one of the largest mission-sending countries in the world, along with Brazil and India.

So, when we as a North American church send missionaries to other parts of the world, we never run alone. As we run with other Christians, we see that we are surrounded by a "cloud of witnesses" from churches and nations everywhere. There is no place for international, cross-cultural missionaries to act as "lone rangers," going it alone and doing their own thing. We are never alone. We no longer do mission *for* or *to* others. We always do mission *with* others.

This in no way means that we cease to do cross-cultural, international mission simply because others are now doing it. Rather, this new reality is a wonderful challenge and inspiration for us to join the marathon and run alongside so many other sisters and brothers committed to sharing the good news of the coming of the kingdom of God in Jesus Christ, in the power of the Holy Spirit. There are over 5.5 billion folks who have not yet experienced the grace of God in Jesus Christ. Together, we live out God's grace and love from everywhere to everywhere, alongside other followers of Jesus.

For the RCA, this fact of a new, truly global mission is easy to understand because of our long history of mission partnerships. In the first chapter of this book, I summarized our unique history of doing global mission through partnerships with local and national churches and institutions. Because of those historic and new mission partnerships, we have Christians from many countries of the world running alongside us, teaching us, encouraging us, working with us. We are not alone in global mission.

The RCA is a relatively small denomination. But it has often partnered with national churches and regional organizations, many of which may have several million members. Because of those partnerships, the RCA, though small, has had an influence locally and globally far beyond its size. Down through its mission history, the RCA has often functioned as a catalyst, calling out, challenging, inspiring, and encouraging much larger denominations and mission organizations in new mission endeavors.

As can be seen in the chapters of this book, the predominant pattern of RCA Global Mission involves doing mission through people and with people. RCA Global Mission is not primarily programmatic or financial. Mission flows through people. That is why we tend to major in sending and supporting long-term intercultural missionaries who build friendships, adopt new languages, and become integral members of their new adopted cultures. Short-term service projects and trips are also important. In our story, many RCA members who got their feet wet in short-term mission experiences ended up devoting a lifetime of service in a missionary situation somewhere in the world.

As we run our mission marathon, we look around us and discover that we are also accompanied by mission-minded RCA pastors, mission task forces, RCA church members, young people from RCA churches and colleges, deacons from many RCA churches, and many women's and men's groups from RCA churches. One of the aspects of RCA mission partnership involves collaboration between the denomination-level mission structures and local RCA congregations. Because of the long-standing "Partner in Mission" support system, there is close cooperation between local RCA congregations and denominational mission structures. Local churches are essential for RCA global missionary activity, and not only because of their financial support. They provide the people, they shape the vision, they are the major source of missionary commitment of the RCA, funneled through the RCA Global Mission structures and staff. Among Protestant denominations in North America, ours is a unique hybrid. Local RCA congregations are the wellspring from which RCA missionary commitment and action flows. Local congregations are intimately involved in the ministry formation, the friendships, and the personal, prayer, and financial support of RCA intercultural missionaries. Simultaneously, the denominational mission structures provide much of the long-term networking, supervision, and personal support of the missionaries. But the wellspring of mission vision and energy flows from the local churches and their members. RCA Global Mission does not run alone. It is always surrounded by its partners.

RCA Global Mission is wholistic[1]

A third characteristic of the DNA of RCA Global Mission is its wholistic approach to doing mission. As we run our Global Mission marathon, we notice that there are dozens of people running alongside us, offering cups of water to drink or pour over our heads if we are hot. They want us to stay healthy. Staying strong and healthy during the marathon involves our spiritual well-being, our mental attitude, our emotional stability, our physical health—our entire being.

Similarly, since the early nineteenth century, RCA Global Mission has been wholistic in its perspective of Christian mission. This

[1] Some spell this word as "holistic." Some people erroneously assume that "holistic" has to do with holiness. "Holistic" and "holiness" are actually unrelated: "holistic/holism" was coined in the 1920s from the Greek *holos* (which means "whole"), while "holy" and "holiness" come from Old English *halig*. So "holistic" already means "whole." I spell the term as "wholistic," derived from "whole," because I want to emphasize our understanding of a gospel of the kingdom that involves a transformation of all of life—personal, social, and structural—not merely one slice of the pie.

view of mission can be appreciated in the stories of the RCA's mission endeavors all over the world.

After World War II, almost all denominations and mission agencies in North America created a great gulf between mission as social action (issues of health, education, agriculture, micro-economics, development, and justice) and mission as evangelism (Bible translation, Bible distribution, church planting, and mostly verbal proclamation of the gospel that invited persons to become followers of Jesus and members of Christian churches). By the 1960s, two separate worlds of mission thought took shape in the U.S. Some advocated almost exclusively social action, while others advocated verbal proclamation seeking conversion to Christian faith. Large organizational structures were created or strengthened to support one or the other of these sides of the picture.

Not so the RCA. Down through its mission history, the RCA has been among a small group of denominations that never split evangelism and social action. We were founding members of the World Council of Churches in 1948 (heavily oriented toward social action) and simultaneously members of the Evangelical Fellowship of Mission Agencies (EFMA, founded in 1946, now known as Missio Nexus) and the Lausanne Movement (both heavily oriented toward verbal, proclamational evangelism). RCA Global Mission has held a view of mission that seeks the broad and deep transformation of all of life. In each context where RCA has been in mission, the RCA missionaries have wrestled with how to balance those two sides of mission. Because of the RCA's commitment to long-term, sensitive, culturally appropriate involvement of missionary personnel with the people among whom they live and work, RCA intercultural missionaries have been involved in agriculture, education, medicine, development, and justice. At the same time, they are witnessing to their faith and inviting women and men to become followers of Jesus Christ and active participants in Christian faith communities. In some areas of the world, this has meant predominantly a ministry of presence, while in other contexts it involved a heavy commitment to Bible translation, Bible distribution, gospel preaching, church planting, and pastoral leadership formation, always accompanied with various types of social action. As summarized in the chapters of this book, in every part of the world where the RCA has been involved in mission, the commitment to wholistic mission can be appreciated.

In January of 2020, RCA Global Mission convened a conference in Florida called "Mission 2020." In Appendix A, I have placed the "RCA Global Mission Principles" that appeared in the conference booklet. Over the three days we were together, we heard from more than 30 RCA Global Mission personnel working in various parts of the world. What was most impressive for me was the down-to-earth, practical, ordinary, realistic, "no-frills," personal way in which they told their stories and explained their mission endeavors. And embedded in all their stories was a view of mission that sought to be wholistic, a gospel of the kingdom adapted to each context that sought the transformation of all of life. They explained how they sought to do mission with, alongside, and in cooperation with the people among whom they live and work.

RCA Global Mission is global

The fourth characteristic of the DNA of RCA Global Mission that flows throughout the chapters of this book is that mission is now *glocal*. As we run our mission marathon, we are accompanied by folks from all over the world who run alongside us toward the finish line. Everyone has the same finish line, regardless of where in the world they came from. This marathon is simultaneously local and global.

The word *glocal* was coined in the 1990s to express this understanding of being simultaneously global and local. The word was first coined by leaders of a web of mega-cities who were studying how global issues impact a mega-city and, simultaneously, how what is happening in a mega-city has immediate global impact. The word *glocal* also arose about the same time in conversations about global internet banking. When I insert my credit card in an ATM, no matter where I am in the world, I access a global banking network. I am at that moment both global and local: *glocal*.

Doing mission today is exactly like that. It is glocal, at once global and local. For example, over 200 languages are spoken in Los Angeles. And there are local Christian congregations where the members speak one—or several—of those languages. Moreover, in any one of those congregations there are members who have family, business, travel, and social connections with others who live in the original home country or in another country somewhere on the globe. These congregations are in fact glocal congregations. What happens in each local congregation has global implications. What happens around the globe has local implications. Christian mission in this new century is glocal. An RCA congregation in western Michigan discovered that. They developed a friendship with a leader from Myanmar (Burma) while that leader was studying at Western Theological Seminary in Holland, Michigan. Now that RCA congregation in Michigan is walking alongside and supporting that leader to plant churches back in Myanmar.

We are in the midst of the largest mass migration of peoples in the history of the earth; Christian leaders, mission agencies, and churches are seeking to understand their missionary role of being a transforming presence in the midst of multiple cultures and multiple religious affiliations. We are seeking to understand what it means to be Christians in mission in religiously and culturally hostile environments around the world.

Furthermore, the largest missionary movement in this century is the migration of Christians from everywhere to everywhere. The Chinese, Korean, African, and Latin American diasporas are now a significant global missionary movement in their own right. This is a global reality that some have described as "polycentric." And the re-evangelization of the West is now part of a new reality that we are just beginning to comprehend. Missionary thought and practice now involve Christian mission from everywhere to everywhere, by everyone to everyone, around the globe in a glocal fashion. Although we have known this for some time, we are just beginning to integrate this new reality into the essence of our missiology.

As we run our marathon, we look toward the finish line seeking to imagine God's future. First and foremost, we are involved in God's mission. Christian mission does not belong to the RCA or to partner churches and organizations around the globe. Fundamentally, it is not our agenda. It belongs to God, who wants to work through God's people to announce the coming of God's kingdom for all peoples, everywhere.

Surrounded by that cloud of witnesses, the author of Hebrews wrote, "Let us fix our eyes on Jesus, the author and perfecter of our faith, who for the joy set before him, endured the cross, despising the shame, and sat down at the right hand of the throne of God" (Hebrews 12:2). Like Jesus, with Jesus, we look toward the finish line when "every knee will bow and every tongue confess that Jesus Christ is Lord, to the glory of God the Father" (Philippians 2:11). Like marathoners, we are challenged to dream bold dreams, looking toward the finish line.

Conclusion

The author of Hebrews challenges us to "run with perseverance the race marked out for us" because we are "surrounded by such a great cloud of witnesses" (Hebrews 12:1). You and I are surrounded by a great cloud of witnesses that includes thousands of women and men of the RCA who have been the agents of God's mission through RCA Global Mission. The cloud includes those who were and are being sent to other places around the globe and those visionary, faithful, and generous women and men, members of RCA congregations, whose vision, commitment, involvement, and support continue to make it possible for the RCA to do global intercultural mission from everywhere to everywhere.

The twenty-first century promises to be the great century of mission. More than 1.5 billion people around the globe profess to be followers of Jesus. Together we speak more languages, we have the Bible translated into more languages, we enjoy the greatest ease of travel and communication than ever before in the history of the human race. For the first time in human history, we can present the gospel in an understandable way (using commercial languages)[2] to every human being on the face of the earth.

Because of our proven ability to partner with other national ministries and churches anywhere and everywhere in the world, God has granted us the blessing of having a large impact for the kingdom of God, far beyond our size and resources. As we seek ways forward in RCA Global Mission, we need to remember and draw inspiration and wisdom from those who have gone before us and seek to live into new ways and forms of RCA mission in the future. We are in the midst of major shifts in understanding and doing Christian mission in this new century. Our way forward is not clear. There are contextual realities in thousands of different situations around the globe that are in constant flux. They challenge us to continually reexamine and reconsider the church's missionary calling.

It is also important to remember that there are certainties that do not change. Our call to participate in God's mission in God's world does not change. My way of saying this is: It is God's will that the church proclaim in word and deed the coming of the kingdom of God in Jesus Christ, inviting women and men, in the power of

---

[2]   In countries like India, Indonesia, or Mexico where many languages are spoken, certain languages are popularly used for commercial buying and selling. Linguists often call these "commercial languages." At present, Christian churches and mission agencies do not have access to all the languages of the world, but in every country, they are able to communicate the gospel through the use of commercial languages.

the Holy Spirit, to become followers of the Lord Jesus Christ, active participants in Christian faith communities, and committed agents of the transformation of their contexts.

May the Holy Spirit grant us insight and wisdom as together we seek ways forward in RCA Global Mission.

For further reading

RCA website: www.rca.org/rca-global-mission

RCA Global Mission. *Field Guide: RCA Missionaries and Partners*. Grand Rapids, MI: Reformed Church in America, 2020.

Afterword

James Hart Brumm

These are amazing and inspiring stories. For over two centuries, women and men from what we now call the Reformed Church in America, working on behalf of the RCA, supported by congregations in places like New Brunswick and South Holland and Albany and North Branch and Pella and Feura Bush and Locust Valley and Fordham Manor and Johnston and Le Mars and Bushkill and Basking Ridge and Lynden and Oostburg and Platte and Stickney and San Antonio and Churchville and Cary and Columbus and Strasburg and Montevideo and Firth and Winnebago and Woodstock, by consistories, women's guilds, Christian endeavor societies, youth fellowships, Bible study groups, and probably a thousand other kinds of names, have done their best to spread the good news of God's love in Christ to people on every corner of this planet. They preached sermons, shared blankets, treated wounds, told stories, built homes and hospitals and relationships, and, in more other ways than this book can share, made the words of Matthew 25 a reality.

These are wonderful stories about RCA mission, but they are not the entire story of RCA mission. How do we know? For one thing,

157

there are sixteen other volumes in the Historical Series of the Reformed Church in America that deal with RCA mission, many of which are mentioned in this book. For another, there are documents in the RCA Archives and other places, such as Samuel Zwemer's diaries, letters home from James Cantine, and dozens of other documents that have been barely touched by scholars. For example, just last September, the Reformed Church Center at New Brunswick Theological Seminary received a scan of a photograph from Geronimo's baptism.[1] Scholars are in regular contact with the RCA Archives with requests to examine our missionary records.[2] This book of essays is a useful, brief overview of the origins of global mission in the RCA. There is so much more to the story.

In 1927, the German physicist Werner Heisenberg put forward the theory that even the observation of a phenomenon inevitably changes the phenomenon.[3] If this is true of mere observation, the long-term interaction of missionaries building relationships and witnessing to the gospel in an alien culture has the potential for even greater unintentional impact. Haruko Wakabiyashi, a member of the faculty in the Asian Languages and Cultures department at Rutgers University, has done research into the cultural effects of RCA (and other) missionaries on Japanese society.[4] Anderson H. M. Jeremiah, lecturer in World Christianity and Religious Studies at Lancaster University, United Kingdom, and a minister of the Church of South India, has examined similar impacts in his homeland.[5] This has also been a concern addressed by Douglas Leonard, former director of RCA Global Mission, who served as coordinator of the Ecumenical United Nations Office in New York City and is now the pastor of the Reformed

[1]   Attachment to an e-mail from William Heydorn to this author, September 1, 2019.
[2]   See the Archivist's reports in the minutes of the Commission on History, RCA, and the *Acts and Proceedings of the General Synod of the Reformed Church in America* for the years 1979 to present.
[3]   Werner Heisenberg, *Physics and Philosophy: The Revolution in Modern Science* (New York: Harper and Row, 1962), 137.
[4]   "Early Impacts: Samurai Responses to Christianity in Nineteenth-Century Japan," an address at the conference "Sent on Ahead: Looking at Groundbreaking Missions in India, Japan, and the Middle East," Monday, November 18, 2019, at New Brunswick Theological Seminary, New Brunswick, New Jersey.
[5]   "American Arcot Mission and its Legacy: An Appraisal," an address at the conference "Sent on Ahead: Looking at Groundbreaking Missions in India, Japan, and the Middle East"; "Caste, Culture, and Christianity," a paper delivered at New Brunswick Theological Seminary on Tuesday, November 19, 2019.

Church in Hopewell, New York.[6] Recordings of all of these scholars are available on the Reformed Church Center page at nbts.edu.

Reformed Christians, heirs of the theology of Augustine and John Calvin, of the Belgic Confession and the Canons of Dort, know that the nature and actions of the church down through the centuries are both heavenly and human, saintly and sinful. We know and freely confess that none of us are without sin, and that sin has fundamentally corrupted everything we do. This is also true of the church's life and work in its local and global ministries and mission. Our missionary impulses were good, and the missionaries we sent into the world meant well. We believe they were guided by God. That does not mean they did not make mistakes. Not all of the unintended or misunderstood results of mission work have been neutral or good.

Here are some examples. In his book *Taking the Jesus Road: The Ministry of the Reformed Church in America Among Native Americans*, LeRoy Koopman discusses, among other things, problems created by the missionaries as they imposed White, European-American culture on Native American students.[7] John Scudder, patriarch of the missionary family who, during nearly two centuries, would contribute over a thousand years of missionary efforts in India, was distrustful of the people whom he had gone to serve and not open to their expressions of faith. In his writing and speaking he often used terms of Western European and Caucasian-American cultural superiority, an attitude that today we would consider racist.[8] The Society of Inquiry Into Missions at New Brunswick Theological Seminary, one of the first such student groups of its kind at US seminaries, inspired generations of RCA missionaries.[9] The members of that society created a museum

---

[6] "The Impact of Christian Missions on Indigenous Peoples," an address at the conference "Sent on Ahead: Looking at Groundbreaking Missions in India, Japan, and the Middle East." The fact that three of these addresses came in the same conference on mission history and the fourth came in a second colloquy, the very next day, is an indication of how seriously this issue is being taken among students of RCA and other global missions.

[7] LeRoy Koopman, *Taking the Jesus Road: The Ministry of the Reformed Church in America Among Native Americans* (Grand Rapids, MI: Eerdmans, 2005).

[8] See, for example, John Scudder, "Appeal to Churches," February 16, 1833, letter in the Archives of the Reformed Church in America.

[9] Luman J. Shafer, in his *History of the Society of Inquiry, 1811–1911* (New Brunswick, New Jersey: The Rev. Archibald Laidlie, D.D., L.L.D. Memorial Fund, 1912), 11–13, notes an 1825 letter from a similar Society at Auburn Seminary which identifies the NBTS Society as the founder of the movement, even though "That the New Brunswick Society had nothing actively to do with the organization of this society at Auburn is certain." Similar societies were formed at several seminaries in the

which—while it never obtained missionary artifacts unethically—was inadvertently responsible for the cultural misappropriation of hundreds of artifacts.[10]

While it can be argued that these actions and behaviors were all appropriate for the times in which they occurred, they were nonetheless products of systemic racism that must be acknowledged and repented of. While we cannot and should not say that the missteps and sins of previous generations in relation to missionary work have outweighed all of the good done by RCA global missionaries, we acknowledge that our missionaries at times did harm to the people whom they were called to serve. Even if such acts and attitudes were unintentional, they still brought disgrace to the cause of Christ, and we need to learn from them as we seek to avoid making similar errors today and tomorrow.

Evaluation and critique are not the purpose of this book. Historically grounded analysis, critique, and evaluation of the RCA's past life and actions are important. Such a book needs to be written. We need to examine all that we have done, including ways that our global mission programs have failed those whom they were called to serve. We need to learn from our mistakes and seek to build a better, more compassionate church. This is how we shall best honor our past and glorify our God.

Celebrate the stories told here. They are a gift to the church. But never forget that these are but the beginning of the story we all need to learn from, for we are all called to serve.

---

eastern United States, and, according to the Society of Inquiry minutes in the NBTS Archives, engaged in regular correspondence with one another. In 1880, the New Brunswick Society was one of three organizers of a gathering of these groups in New York. In 1881, the Inter-Seminary Alliance met in New Brunswick, with 27 schools represented by 250 delegates; this group eventually became the Theological Department of the Young Men's Christian Association (Shafer, 36–37).

[10] Shafer, *History of the Society of Inquiry*, 35ff. See also "Notes on the Bussing Museum," unpublished manuscript in Gardner A. Sage Library.

APPENDIX

RCA Global Mission Principles[1]

The world has changed dramatically since the early days of the modern missionary movement. Today, more than 70 percent of all Christians live in the southern hemisphere. North America is increasingly a secular society and a mission field in need of the good news of Jesus Christ. Though our strategies and tools may change, the mission principles that have served the Reformed Church in America so well over the past 350+ years continue to do so today.

Respectful witness

We believe we are a global covenant family united in Christ and living as incarnational Christian witnesses who are called to exist in harmony with diverse societies, traditions, and cultures.

Long-term mutual relationships

We believe in a purposeful and undeviating focus on mission collaboration and interdependency that matures into deep-rooted cooperation and significant partnership.

---

[1]   RCA Global Mission, *Field Guide: RCA Missionaries and Partners* (Grand Rapids, MI: Reformed Church in America, 2020), 17.

Holistic engagement

We believe in a global, reformational vision of God's kingdom in which we engage a fallen creation through the power and nature of Christ.

Sustainable empowerment

We believe in breaking the cycle of foreign dependency and paternalism by promoting interdependent, Christ-centered cooperatives that culminate in locally sufficient, locally supported, and locally sustainable, faithful transformation.